HAROLD PINTER:
You Never Heard Such Silence

HAROLD PINTER:
You Never Heard Such Silence

edited by
Alan Bold

VISION
and
BARNES & NOBLE

Vision Press Limited
Fulham Wharf
Townmead Road
London SW6 2SB

and

Barnes & Noble Books
81 Adams Drive
Totowa, NJ 07512

ISBN (UK) 0 85478 495 0
ISBN (US) 0 389 20535 4

Printed and bound in Great Britain by
Unwin Brothers Ltd.,
Old Woking, Surrey.
Phototypeset by Galleon Photosetting,
Ipswich, Suffolk.
MCMLXXXIV

Contents

Introduction

by ALAN BOLD

Harold Pinter's dramatic output is, by general agreement, uniquely expressive. Though the influence of Beckett and others has been cited in critical comments, Pinter remains an original with a tone so unusual that it has brought the epithet 'Pinteresque' into being to describe an atmosphere of expectation. Admittedly Pinter himself detests the term. When it was put to him, in a *Paris Review* interview of 1966, he was unimpressed:

> That word! These damn words and that word 'Pinteresque' particularly—I don't know what they're bloody well talking about! I think it's a great burden for me to carry, and for other writers to carry. . . . I'm just a writer; and I think that I've been overblown tremendously because there's a dearth of really fine writing, and people tend to make too much of a meal

Pinter has always been reluctant to discuss his plays in terms of their extra-theatrical meaning and each performance of a Pinter play reveals the reason for this. Every Pinter play is a dramatic text that defines its own context, for the action invariably unfolds in an autonomous state of uncertainty. What the characters do in a Pinter play is seemingly self-contained and only acknowledges the outside world obliquely; in *The Birthday Party* (1958) the identity of Goldberg and McCann is exactly what they do in the play. When Pinter's curtain comes down the situation is resolved, theatrically, until the next production. More than any of his contemporaries, Pinter is a complete man of the theatre.

His biographical background, of course, is clearly histrionic. When the *Paris Review* interviewer asked him about his

7

profession Pinter replied 'Oh, yes, [acting] was all I ever did.' He is not theatrical in the debased sense of the term which equates the actor with over-the-top camping; he is genuinely theatrical in that he invents according to the craft he knows best and is most easily moved by the magic of performance. When describing his technical methods Pinter often speaks in a matter-of-fact manner but he can rise majestically to the occasion when recalling a great moment on the stage. In 'Mac', his tribute to his friend Anew McMaster, he enthuses over the transformation of colleague into stage character:

> Sometimes, late at night, after the show, [Mac] looked very old. But on stage in *Othello* he stood, well over six foot, naked to the waist, his gestures complete, final, nothing jagged, his move-ment of the utmost fluidity and yet of the utmost precision: stood there, dead in the centre of the role, and the great sweeping symphonic playing would begin, the rare tension and release within him, the arrest, the swoop, the savagery, the majesty and repose.

There is, throughout Pinter's work, a quintessentially histrionic attitude. In a Pinter play the characters act ritualistically rather than realistically; they play out their roles and do not so much engage in conversation as speak in set-pieces. Each statement is theatrically effective because all the facts of Pinter's life have been perceived dramatically. Of the genesis of *The Birthday Party* he said, to the *Paris Review* interviewer:

> *The Birthday Party* had . . . been in my mind for a long time. It was sparked off from a very distinct situation in digs when I was on tour . . . I was in those digs, and this woman was Meg in the play, and there was a fellow staying there in Eastbourne, on the coast. The whole thing remained with me, and three years later I wrote the play.

As an actor he remade a real situation in a theatrical image. For Pinter the world is raw material for the stage. Indeed he said, on being awarded the 1970 German Shakespeare Prize, 'I have referred to facts, by which I mean theatrical facts'. When he began as a dramatist he was an actor married to an actress (Vivien Merchant). The rich verbal texture of Pinter's theatrical routine is inspired, I believe, by the experience of spending long hours in rehearsal where every utterance is under scrutiny and has to be delivered with dramatic impact. Pinter's concession to naturalism is an unusual one for it comes perfectly naturally to him, as an actor, to think of characters speaking only when they have something extraordinary to say. The play is, undoubtedly, the thing for Pinter which is why he said, to the National Student Drama Festival in Bristol in 1962,

> What I write has no obligation to anything other than to itself. My responsibility is not to audiences, critics, producers, directors, actors or to my fellow men in general, but to the play in hand, simply.

Whereas critics have frequently been confused by Pinter's work, it is notable that actors have little trouble comprehending a particular play since they accept the text as a theatrical score they have to translate into vocal terms. John Normington, who played Sam in the first production of *The Homecoming* (1965), observed that 'What Pinter wanted to stress . . . was a stylized naturalism. It was in fact natural speech rhythms. That is the way people talk.' Paul Rogers— Max in the same production, also quoted in John and Anthea Lahr's *Casebook* (1971) on *The Homecoming*—was also aware of the theatrical import of the play:

> [It was necessary] to be utterly arrogant and sure of the play, of yourself and your own skill as a player. This is very valuable. It's the kind of thing that your intuitive star, the kind that just blazes there, has. They possess an arrogance, which is often very, very charming. It's so marvellous because nobody else has it. Ordinary people in the street don't have it.

The implication of these remarks is that Pinter is a professional man of the theatre who communicates with actors in a direct way because of their inside knowledge of his art. On the other hand the audience is not emotionally drawn into the action, but distanced from the actors—excluded from action that breaks the behavioural rules of society in the interests of an inner theatrical logic. Pinter does not involve the audience so much as impose a theatrical spectacle on it. Moreover, Pinter's characters do not simulate the kind of acts an audience would regard as normal; the actors are directed to interact with each other in the most theatrically effective way. For this reason Pinter-criticism goes sadly wrong when commentators claim to know more than Pinter has put into a play, when they speculate on the extra-theatrical activities of the characters.

In his Bristol speech of 1962 Pinter emphasized how firmly his characters are fixed in a purely theatrical dimension:

> I suggest there can be no hard distinctions between what is real and what is unreal, nor between what is true and what is false. A thing is not necessarily either true or false; it can be both true and false. A character on the stage who can present no convincing argument or information as to his past experience, his present behaviour or his aspirations, nor give a comprehensive analysis of his motives is as legitimate and as worthy of attention as one who, alarmingly, can do all these things.

What Pinter projects then, is not an imitation of reality but a theatrical extension of reality. He opens with an ordinary situation—breakfast in a seaside resort or a family altercation in a London house—and pursues it to an astonishing conclusion. In the process Pinter expresses his comic vision of life by linguistic means that exploit the resources of the stage. He is adept, for instance, at ridiculing the potentially sublime. In *A Slight Ache* (1959) Edward is caught in the act of pontificating pretentiously:

> FLORA. Which essay?
> EDWARD. My essay on space and time.
> FLORA. But . . . I've never . . . I don't know that one.
> EDWARD. You don't know it?
> FLORA. I thought you were writing one about the Belgian Congo.
> EDWARD. I've been engaged on the dimensionality and continuity of space . . . and time . . . for years.

Lenny, the pimp of *The Homecoming*, is the one who ruminates philosophically while the academic doctor of philosophy, Teddy, reacts with indifference:

> LENNY. Well, look at it this way . . . you don't mind my asking you some questions, do you?
> TEDDY. If they're within my province.
> LENNY. Well, look at it this way. How can the unknown merit

reverence? In other words, how can you revere that of which you're ignorant? At the same time it would be ridiculous to propose that what we *know* merits reverence. What we know merits any one of a number of things, but it stands to reason reverence isn't one of them. In other words, apart from the known and the unknown, what else is there?

    Pause.

    TEDDY. I'm afraid I'm the wrong person to ask.

In *No Man's Land* (1975) the thuggish Briggs suddenly breaks into culture:

    SPOONER. The boss . . . is a poet himself?

    BRIGGS. Don't be silly. He's more than that, isn't he? He's an essayist and critic as well. He's a man of letters.

Subsequently Briggs launches into another mode of discourse with regard to Spooner:

    BRIGGS. To him? To a pisshole collector? To a shithouse operator? To a jamrag vendor? What the fuck are you talking about? Look at him. He's a mingejuice bottler, a fucking shitcake baker. What are you talking to him for?

Flora and Edward and Teddy and Lenny and Spooner and Briggs develop, before the eyes (and ears) of an audience, because the language they use has a life of its own. Linguistically, Pinter does not transcribe conversational commonplaces but organizes speech artistically to give the theatrical illusion of everyday discourse. His finest characters have an unforgettable verbal presence.

    Pinter's status as the supreme stage artist of his time has been acknowledged by several critics. In *The Language of Modern Drama* (1977) Gareth Lloyd Evans notes 'One very important facet of [Pinter's uniqueness] is that the language is eminently written for the actor—he is a player's playwright—as a kind of code'. Simon Trussler, too, concludes *The Plays of Harold Pinter* (1973) with the observation that 'Pinter is, then, an actor's playwright, with all the virtues and limitations that implies.' Yet the assumption that quintessentially theatrical writing is somehow limited leads Trussler to some extremely indignant value judgements. Of *The Homecoming*, Trussler writes:

    The Homecoming is, in short, a modishly intellectualised melodrama, its violence modulated by its vagueness, its emotional stereotyping disguised by carefully planted oddities of juxta-position and expression. To suspend disbelief in this play is to call a temporary halt to one's humanity . . . *The Homecoming* is [Pinter's] only work by which I have felt myself actually soiled and diminished. If a work is pornographic because it toys with the most easily manipulated human emotions—those of sex and (more especially) violence—without pausing to relate cause and effect, then *The Homecoming* can even be said to fall into such a category. . . . Here, Pinter's enterprise is sick, and each thing melts in mere, unmotivated oppugnancy.

Trussler's diatribe is motivated by a suspicion that Pinter is playing games with his audience and that this is a disreputable thing for a dramatist to do. Unlike Trussler, I do not believe there is anything intrinsically restricting in being 'a player's playwright' or 'an actor's playwright'; surely the precedent of actor-writer Shakespeare is evidence of that. Nor do I believe that Pinter is an amoralist obsessed by violence. Trussler completely misses the comic point of the play and seems unable to see that when characters offer verbal violence to each other the purpose of such exchanges is to extend the imagery implicit in the drama.

Max, in *The Homecoming*, is one of Pinter's most glorious creations. Throughout the play he uses violent images that explore his given background as a butcher. Now Pinter obviously finds butchers creatures of high comedy: his revue sketch 'That's All' (1964) has Mrs A and Mrs B discussing butchers. Early on in *The Homecoming* Max tells Lenny 'I'll chop your spine off' which establishes an image Pinter subse-quently puts to great comic effect. After an argument with his brother Sam, Max launches into a eulogy of his profession:

> Well, I'll tell you one thing. I respected my father not only as a man but as a number one butcher! And to prove it I followed him into the shop. I learned to carve a carcass at his knee. I commemorated his name in blood. I gave birth to three grown men! All on my own bat. What have you done?

Here the comedy is achieved by contrasting Max's senti-mental attachment to his trade with the physical images of carcass and blood. When Max addresses Ruth he again alternates between emotional self-indulgence and factual references to his work. Explaining, with heavy dramatic irony, that his wife Jessie taught 'those boys' (a pimp, a bruiser, an academic who abandons his wife) 'all the morality they know' Max waxes lyrically before waning brutally:

> That woman was the backbone to this family. I mean, I was busy working twenty-four hours a day in the shop, I was going all over the country to find meat, I was making my way in the world, but I left a woman at home with a will of iron, a heart of gold and a mind. [. . .] I worked as a butcher all my life, using the chopper and the slab, the slab, you know what I mean, the chopper and the slab! To keep my family in luxury. [. . .] A crippled family, three bastard sons, a slutbitch of a wife—don't talk to me about the pain of childbirth—I suffered the pain, I've still got the pangs—when I give a little cough my back collapses [. . .]

Max amounts to the language he employs. When he goes on about his days as a butcher he communicates comically since the grim ritual of the work undermines his professional romanticism; when he indulges in pathological outbursts ('Take that disease away from me') he is the embodiment of unwholesomeness. He is a dynamic creation not a static instrument for amplifying the author's opinions. Pinter, it is clear, exploits the possibilities of his medium like nobody else.

Pinter's plays are the dramatic realisation of a genuine artistic gift yet some critics seek to explain them away as if the dramatist was using all his ingenuity to disguise some mysterious philosophical message that lurks between the lines—perhaps in the pauses. Some critical comments have been confused because the critics have not been able to receive the play as the author intended it. Whereas actors and audiences have found themselves at ease in the oral element of an actual performance, critics have frequently agonised over a play as if it existed only on paper as a puzzle awaiting an analytical solution. For such critics the purely textual approach has led to spurious suppositions. Gareth Lloyd Evans, for example, claims that Pinter is primarily a poet:

> He is poetic in the deeper sense that no specific and clear literal meaning can be abstracted from the majority of his plays . . . Pinter is not concerned with the actualities of man in society but, taking on the traditional functions of the poet, with some of the realities of what man is. He uses, as many poets have done,

13

the sense-data of the contemporary world as a sharp salt, but it is no more.

Pinter is not, though, a poet manqué using his fundamental talent in an alien form. He is a dramatist who uses an acquired skill to express an instinctively comic vision of humanity. His humour, admittedly, is often black and his turn of phrase deliberately sinister. Nevertheless his plays remake life in an elaborately theatrical image—which is what all the great masters of comedy have done.

Another failure of much Pinter-criticism is that it makes the mistake of being morose about passages that are evidently intended humorously. Pinter's people are funny characters who come out with amusing lines as they go about their verbal business. Think of Meg, in *The Birthday Party*, who feels the word 'succulent' should never be said 'to a married woman', or the following exchange in the same play:

> PETEY. Someone's just had a baby.
> MEG. Oh, they haven't! Who?
> PETEY. Some girl.
> MEG. Who, Petey, who?
> PETEY. I don't think you'd know her.
> MEG. What's her name?
> PETEY. Lady Mary Splatt.
> MEG. I don't know her.

Think of Gus and Ben in *The Dumb Waiter* (1960) discussing whether one lights the kettle or the gas. Think of Edward, in *A slight Ache*, offering a catalogue of drinks to a mute matchseller:

> Now look, what will you have to drink? A glass of ale. Curacao Fockink orange? Ginger beer? Tia Maria? A Wachenheimer Fuchsmantel Reisling Beeren Auslese? Gin and it? Chateauneuf-du-Pape? A little Asti Spumante? Or what do you say to a straightforward Piesporter Goldtropfschen Feine Auslese (Reichsgraf von Kesselstaff)? Any preference?

Think of Lenny's problem with ticking noises ('I'm not all that convinced it was the clock') in *The Homecoming* or Duff's erudite asides on draught beer in *Landscape* (1968). These examples have the verbal incongruity of knockabout farce as does the following exchange between Spooner and Briggs in *No Man's Land*:

14

SPOONER. Yes. The landlord is a friend of mine. It is on that account that he has favoured us with a private room. It is true of course that I informed him Lord Lancer would be attending the meeting. He at once appreciated that a certain degree of sequesteredness would be the order of the day.
BRIGGS. Lord Lancer?
SPOONER. Our patron.
BRIGGS. He's not one of the Bengal Lancers, is he?
SPOONER. No, no. He's of Norman descent.

Pinter is frequently happy to send life up for theatrical effect. Verbally, his characters are larger than life and so can effortlessly alternate between lyrical fantasies and downright nastiness. The characters are as compelling as the language Pinter commands with such dramatic expertise.

If Pinter's vision is, as I have suggested, fundamentally funny then he is also aware that comedy is most movingly conveyed when it contains pathos. There is a terrible pathos in the defeatist antics of Spooner in *No Man's Land*: intellectually he longs for recognition as a poet yet Briggs recognizes him only as 'a pintpot attendant in The Bull's Head. And a pisspot attendant as well'. *The Caretaker* (1960) operates by making three pathetic characters keep each other's company. Max, in *The Homecoming*, is a pathetic old man who dwells on the distant days when he was a tearaway with his friend Mac:

> Huhh! We were two of the worst hated men in the West End of London. I tell you, I still got the scars. We'd walk into a place, the whole room'd stand up, they'd make way to let us pass. You never heard such silence.

Max is a memorable theatrical creation. If a member of a theatre audience met the likes of Max in 'real life', he would find him intolerable. On stage, though, Max is a figure of fun who simultaneously invokes the pathos of old age. The verbal humour of Pinter enchants the audience, while the pathos makes a Pinter play a profoundly human statement. Pinter's comedic genius has much in common with Chaplin's; every flash of humour illuminates the human condition. The comparison may seem odd since Chaplin's medium was the silence of the early cinema whereas Pinter's medium is the sound of the stage. Still, both men make great comedy from circumstances that would seem dismal in real life.

Because of his histrionic integrity Pinter is able to persuade the spectator to share his vision. It is interesting, for example, that Noel Coward began by dismissing Pinter as 'completely incomprehensible and insultingly boring' (Diary of 27 March 1960) but was soon (Diary of 2 May 1960) saluting 'a genuine original. I don't think he could write in any other way if he tried. . . . *Nothing* happens except that somehow it does. The writing is at moments brilliant and quite unlike anyone else's.' It is a measure of Pinter's greatness that he has the dramatic power to convert the sceptical to his special qualities. A 'genuine original', he is therefore a difficult writer to classify and this book celebrates his variety while investigating his stylistic repertoire. What all the contributors have in common is a fascination with Pinter's art and an admiration for an author who seems, at times, to articulate the ineffable. This book contends that the finest Pinter plays have something vital to say—or, at least, to suggest, for Pinter is a subtle dramatist. He places words carefully in a highly theatrical structure so there is every point in listening to what happens creatively between the lines: you never heard such silence.

Acknowledgements: for permission to use illustrative quotations from the published work of Harold Pinter, the editor wishes to thank Harold Pinter; Harold Pinter's sole agent Actac (Theatrical and Cinematic) Ltd., 16 Cadogan Lane, London SW1; and Eyre Methuen Ltd.

Part One:
POINTS OF REFERENCE

1

Directing Pinter

by PETER HALL

I can speak about how I work on a Pinter play. It doesn't mean to say this is *the way*. And I must make absolutely clear that although Harold and I have had a long association and I've directed a number of his stage plays, and we've worked together on films and so on, it is a totally pragmatic situation. I would hate anybody reading this to think *this is the way to direct Pinter*. This absolutely is not true; it's the way *I* direct Pinter. Having said that, my working arrangement with him has been, over the years, that in front of the actors—and I stress that—he can say anything he likes about what I'm doing, and the production, and the rights and wrongs of it. And in front of the actors I can say anything I like about the text, and the rights and wrongs of that. But I am the final arbiter of the production, and he, obviously, is the final arbiter of the text. I think this has, on occasion, been very tough on the actors, because we do develop a kind of Tweedledum and Tweedledee act, and we are, I think, very good for each other. But that doesn't necessarily mean we're very good for some of the actors surrounding us. It's all a bit high-powered, it's very wordy, and we split hairs with great glee. The scrutiny can get a bit much. But Harold will never say, 'You should do *that*.' He will say, 'That isn't right', which is something quite different.

Let's take *The Homecoming*. The problem there is that the biggest bastard in a house full of bastards is actually the man who at first sight appears to be the victim—that is, Teddy, the

19

brother who brings his wife home. He is actually locked in a battle of wills with his father and with his brothers, and of course, with his wife, during which, in some sense, he destroys his wife, and his family, and his father, and himself, rather than give in. He is actually the protagonist. Now, it's very easy for an actor to fall into the 'martyred' rôle in that part, because Teddy says so little—just sits there while all the other characters are speculating about his wife's qualities in bed. But this is the point—it's a tremendous act of will on his part to take it, and if he was actually feeling anything uncontrolled, he wouldn't be able to do it.

It wasn't until Michael Jayston did it in the film that I realized how hard Teddy actually had to be, and how much in control he was. I'd felt it, but I hadn't pushed it far enough. And Harold was always saying to me, during the two stage productions, 'That's not quite right.'

He would indicate that one should make it harder, but we never found the way. I don't want to denigrate Michael Bryant or Michael Craig who played the part on the stage. I think it was something to do with the personalities of the particular actors concerned, who are giving off vibrations which they may not know about, and which one has to allow for in certain ways. So my approach to a Pinter play is first of all to try and expose the underlying melodrama of the text. I try and find out who does hate who, and who loves who, and who's doing what to whom, and in the first stage of rehearsals play it very crudely.

Why, in *The Homecoming*, is Lenny so obsessed from the word go with destroying his father? Talking about his cooking and his rotten meals and so on. Now that must not, in my view, be played with any kind of heaviness; but the underlying feeling is one of absolute naked hatred. Because I think at the base of a good deal of Harold's work is the cockney game of taking the piss; and part of that game is that you should not be quite sure whether the piss is being taken or not. In fact, if you know I'm taking the piss, I'm not really doing it very well; and a good deal of Harold's tone has to do with that very veiled kind of mockery.

Now, actors can't play veiling until they know what they're veiling, so we play mockery, we play hatred, we play animosity, we play the extreme black-and-white terms of a character. That stage of rehearsal is very crude, but it's a very important stage, because unless the actor understands what game he is playing, what his actual underlying motivations are, the ambiguity of the text will mean nothing. People who think that all you've got to do in Pinter is to say it, hold the pause and then say the next line, are wrong. The mystery to me is that there is a communication in the theatre which is beyond words, and which is actually concerned with direct feeling. An actor who says to you, 'All right, I may be feeling that, but unless I show the audience that I'm feeling it, they won't understand', is actually wrong. If he feels it and masks it, the audience still gets it.

Because he has such a distinctive voice, very quickly there came to be a 'Pinter style', which is external. Actors know you speak Pinter in a dry, clipped way, and you hold the pause, and you don't inflect very much, and you don't show very much emotion. It's wrong, of course—a convention, nothing more. Like saying play Chekhov sad, or Shakespeare with a lot of lung power. But, very early on, one felt actors making Pinter patterns, and that's really dreadful—though I suppose it's better than actors trying to 'normalize' Pinter's speech rhythms, because the first thing I say to actors when we're beginning a Pinter play is 'Look, don't mislead yourselves into thinking that if there's a pause there, there shouldn't be a pause there, or, if there's a silence, there shouldn't be a silence, because there should. Our job is to find out why. And don't, in order to make it comfortable, turn a full-stop into a comma, or break it up in a colloquial way different to the way he's written it.'

I actually believe that Beckett and Pinter are poetic dramatists, in the proper sense of the word; they have a linear structure and a formal structure which you'd better just observe—don't learn it wrong, don't speak it wrong, you can't, you mustn't. But there are various things that you can exercise. One of the greatest influences on Pinter, obviously, is the early Eliot—particularly in the repeated phrase, the catching up of a phrase and repeating it over three sentences, keeping it up in the air, like a ball. Now, that is often written in three separate sentences; but it has to make a unit, and you don't find that unit till about the third week. So at the beginning it is better just to observe absolutely accurately what he's written.

I also know that the intensity of the feeling underlying Pinter's text is so very extreme, so very brutal, that you have to explore this melodramatic area that I was speaking about. And this of course raises the question of where the actors live in relation to each other, physically, because until you start letting loose the naked feeling, you don't know the answers to very basic questions, such as, are eyes necessary, or are they not? Are they part of the weaponry?

My vocabulary is all the time about hostility and battles and weaponry, but that is the way Pinter's characters operate, as if they were all stalking round a jungle, trying to kill each other, but trying to disguise from one another the fact that they are bent on murder. And whether you can see a character's face or whether you can't, whether you hold his eyes or not, is absolutely critical—and that to a very large extent comes out of the actor's psyche, once the feelings are being generated. So I wouldn't have anything to say about the physical life of a Pinter play until the emotions had been released, because I wouldn't know what they should be. Equally, Pinter deals in stillness, in confrontations which are unbroken, and I believe it mandatory to do as few moves in a Pinter play as possible. You don't want moves up to the drinks cabinet, or across to the table, in order to 'break it up', or to make it seem naturalistic. It isn't naturalistic.

Pinter has got a terrific selectivity about physical life on the stage. His stage directions, if he needs to give them, about where people move and what they do, are extremely precise, and if he doesn't give them, it's just as well to assume nothing is necessary. This also goes for design. If the set for *The Homecoming* is a naturalistic representation of a house in North London, then the glass of water makes almost no impression, because it's one glass among many knick-knacks. I think one of the troubles about *The Birthday Party* as a play was that Pinter hadn't yet achieved in formal terms the absolute clarity of his vision. *The Birthday Party* exists in that rather cluttered room; it's all more unnecessarily naturalistic.

* * *

I like, by the end of the first ten days, to be able to have a melodramatic run-through, with books in hand—something which is very emotional and very, very crude. The next stage actually is to try to analyse exactly what games of hostility each character is playing with the others. Because they all play games, all the time. They all tease each other, they all try and get rises out of each other, they all try and disturb each other by saying the opposite of what the other one was hoping or expecting. This reaches its obvious climax in *Landscape,* where one character is apparently totally oblivious of the other, although she obviously hears every word he says.

One of the worrying things for actors in Pinter is that you can never trust what is said to be literally true. It is much safer, in fact, to assume that it is a ploy, rather than the truth, unless you can actually discover that it is the truth. So when the actors have found how to wear their hearts on their sleeves and actually show their emotions, you then have to start a process where they hide their emotions, because to show emotion in Pinter's world is a weakness, which is mercilessly punished by the other characters. You have to construct the mask of the character—because all Pinter's characters have masks—though it's no good having a mask unless you know what's underneath it. But the mask almost never slips. It's exactly like that Marceau mime, where he's laughing, and the mask gets stuck in the grin, and you know his heart is breaking underneath. Now, his breaking heart is what you feel, but he doesn't actually indicate that his heart is breaking at all. That's very like acting in Pinter

So the second stage is to find how to disguise the emotions which are quite evidently being felt. When Ruth returns with Teddy and comes downstairs in the morning and the father is so dreadful to her and to his son, 'having tarts in the house at night', the obvious realistic response would be to break down left and bury your head in the sofa, or whatever. But he beckons her over to him, the father does, and she crosses and looks him in the eye, and he says to her, 'How many kids have you got?' 'Three.' 'All yours, Ted?' Now, by any normal standards of improvization, Ruth should be playing that scene hysterically, but she isn't. The alarm is underneath, but totally masked.

She's taking the old man on. If the old man is making that kind of challenge, she is accepting it. It doesn't mean to say she's not upset, underneath her mask, just as in the last section of the play, when Teddy is deliberately pushing the family, they retaliate with the proposition that his wife should be put on the game, as a dreadful joke at first, to see if he'll crack. And he is saying throughout the last twenty minutes of the play, 'You live your joke. Go on. You want to put her on the game? You needn't think I'll object. *Put* her on the game.' He's dying inside, because he doesn't, of course, want to lose his wife. But again, the mask is not allowed to slip.

There's one little crack at the end of the play, the most difficult moment of the play, when he's leaving the room, and Ruth says, 'Don't become a stranger.' It is very difficult to play. That's the first and only time she calls him Eddie, which is obviously the intimate and familiar name. It is all there, and it's all very . . . calculated is the wrong word, because I know Harold to be a deeply instinctive writer, who writes very quickly once it's there to be written, and it would not be true to say that he works it all out like an intellectual game.

You have to direct two plays each time you direct a Pinter play. And I think the achievement of a Pinter production must be that the two plays meet. Because what stirs the audience is not the mask, not the control, but what is underneath it: that's what upsets them, that's what terrifies and moves them. In that sense Pinter's is a new form of theatre. It's very difficult to point to anybody else and say, 'That's the way he operates too.' Beckett, of course, sometimes.

I do think that Harold has recognized from the beginning of his writing that if, say, I'm sitting in this room on my own, I'm in a totally relaxed state—I don't know how my face is behaving. I'm not concerned about it, I'm not presenting myself to anybody. A knock on the door, by you, is sufficient to make my face form a pattern, even before you've actually entered, and from that moment on neither of us, either by word or by deed or in physical relation to each other, are expressing what we are actually feeling. We are modifying ourselves in relation to each other, and all the modifications, the signals of modern behaviour, are aimed at preserving the mask. We are playing a game—that is, social intercourse.

Pinter has worked from that premise, and taken very dreadful situations, usually, dreadful confrontations between people, which are about territorial battles, or battles over people. And where Pinter on the stage goes wrong is if the actors stop playing the game, if they actually show what they're feeling, because it becomes ludicrous—you know, those unfortunate laughs you can get in Pinter when it's played without underlying truth. Suddenly, something quite apparently serious is said, which pulls the rug away from everything. Now, Pinter *is* very funny, mainly because you can't believe people can maintain these signals, these masks, and it's so shocking, it makes you laugh. But if an actor indulges himself and actually drops the mask, and says, 'I want to show the audience that I'm breaking my heart', the whole scene collapses.

I think it's at this point, as you manufacture the masks, that you have to verify, in a very particular way, that you are saying what Pinter says, and hitting the rhythms that he wrote. It's no good doing it earlier, because then you apply it like a funny hat to the actor. But once the play is beginning to live, you cannot be too meticulous. What Pinter wrote is always better than what a lazy actor will come up with. Now, this may seem a very small and pedantic point, but most of our actors have a fairly easy-going, not to say contemptuous, attitude to what a dramatist has written, and for the average playwright, writing the average colloquial flim-flam, it doesn't much matter whether you say 'but' instead of 'and', or put in a few extra words. It does in Pinter, and it is excruciatingly difficult to get it completely accurate. But *when* you get it accurate, then the rhythm—and he has the most astonishing ability to write rhythms—begins to work. And you begin to feel the emotions underlying those rhythms. Let me put it like this. If you sing a Mozart aria correctly, certain responses begin to be necessary inside you. Now, you could say that's putting the cart before the horse, but that's the way it is—you're not improvising something of your own, you're singing some notes of Mozart. It's much the same with Pinter.

You can do that too early, and then you simply have the actor imitating surface rules. He must already be alive in himself, emotionally, otherwise it's an imposition. But there has to come a point—and this is the most unpleasant, agonizing moment of rehearsal—when you actually get it right. It's not easy.

There is a difference in Pinter between a pause and a silence and three dots. A pause is really a bridge where the audience think that you're this side of the river, then when you speak again, you're the other side. That's a pause. And it's alarming, often. It's a gap, which retrospectively gets filled in. It's not a dead stop—that's a silence, where the confrontation has become so extreme, there is nothing to be said until either the temperature has gone down, or the temperature has gone up, and then something quite new happens. Three dots is a very tiny hesitation, but it's there, and it's different from a semi-colon, which Pinter almost never uses, and it's different from a comma. A comma is something that you catch up on, you go through it. And a full stop's just a full stop. You stop.

I think a Pinter play usually needs about five or six weeks. One of the reasons why it needs a long time is that a concentrated Pinter rehearsal is so exhausting for actors they can't take more than about four hours a day without actually cheating for the fifth or sixth, or just getting so taut that it doesn't work. Four to five hours a day is about the maximum they can take.

The ideal way to work on a Pinter play would be to rehearse it for three weeks, and then design the set. Of course, we're never in that situation. I've only been able to do that once in my life, and that was for an Albee production. When it comes to sets, costumes, props, I think everything burns itself so strongly on the audience's mind in a Pinter play that the coffee cup really has to be very carefully considered. It sounds very fanciful, but the apples in *The Homecoming* had to be green— they could not be yellow or red, because they simply didn't disturb visually. The moment when Sam picks up the apple and eats it and says, 'Feeling a bit peckish' to the old man, is a kick in the crutch to him, and a soft yellow apple would not have had the effect. I sound obsessive, I am. The furniture, the costumes, are very, very carefully scrutinized and a lot of things change, until one builds up something where one can

26

feel that each second is charged with something, and is right.

The artist that I have thought about visually for Pinter, ever since I read *The Birthday Party*, is Magritte—that hard-edged, very elegant, very precise style. Again, you see, you can't overstate. I remember in *Old Times* initially Vivien Merchant's Anna had a very elegant, rather warm reddish dress. It *wasn't* red, it was reddish, but it made a total statement of the Scarlet Woman as soon as she walked on to the stage, and it had to be changed for that reason. Pinter deals in masks in every sense, every person watching the play feels slightly different about it, and you shouldn't pre-empt anybody's solutions.

The most difficult thing of all comes when you meet the audience, because a Pinter actor has to control the audience in a quite deliberate way. It requires a degree of control in the actor, a degree of arrogance in the actor, towards the audience. For instance, you need to let an audience laugh in Pinter, so that at the precise moment when they have laughed themselves out, you can hit them hard with the actuality. The plays are constructed like that, and it has to do with that tenth part of the actor's mind, which has got nothing to do with truth, but with control and technique—the tenth of you standing outside and watching the whole thing. You have to be absolutely adroit.

Audiences are not that erratic for Pinter, actually. I think the precision is the instrument of control, and you can slightly increase the pause, or slightly increase the length of a laugh in order to grip a particular audience. Pinter audiences get off the hook and laugh at people as objects if you don't control them. You really have to make them listen, you really do have to hear that pin drop, and that takes a degree of expertise in the actor which is, I think, pretty considerable. But all the time, the paradox remains, about this intensity of feeling. That has to be utterly true. Because I have seen my own productions of Pinter, without the actors being aware of it, dry out in a fortnight or three weeks, so that the level of intensity under-lying the masks has dropped, and actually what is being seen is a very chic series of patterns.

*   *   *

27

So far, I think Harold has brought back into the theatre well-honed words which are not pretentious, and are not gilded and are not sequined. I think he has brought poetic drama back into the theatre. I think he has made words—the scrutiny of words, the use of words—serious again in the theatre, which for too long had thought of poetic drama as a sort of fancy hat you put on. You wanted to say something ordinary, but because it was poetic drama you put on a funny hat.

Speaking personally, I get a very bleak, very uncompromising, very hostile view of life out of him. Counterbalanced by a longing for contact and relation and . . . not getting into a situation of deep regrets, which is very painful. Because all his characters do have regrets, do crucify themselves, and everybody else. But I think what is for me wonderful about Pinter is that in an unblinkingly hostile situation where everybody does go wrong in some way or another, there are little moments of light and tenderness which are cherished. He is a very pessimistic dramatist; but I don't really understand how anybody could honestly be writing in the 1960s or 1970s and be particularly sunny. People are always saying to me, 'Why don't you do happy plays, that are life-enhancing?' to which the answer is 'Well, why don't people write them?' But I find the great thing about him is that his tenderness and his compassion are not sentimental, but absolutely, unblinkingly accurate.

NOTE

This contribution is based on a series of responses to questions put by Catherine Itzin and Simon Trussler. The complete interview, 'Directing Pinter', is in *Theatre Quarterly*, Vol. IV, No. 16, November 74–January 75.

2

Harold Pinter—Innovator?

by RANDALL STEVENSON

Pinter an innovator? Never. Critics and theatre-goers have been too ready to evade the challenges and apparent mysteries of his plays by over-emphasizing Pinter's originality, suggesting that he is hard to assess and understand partly because nothing quite like him has been seen before.[1] Pinter is not well served by this prevalent critical assumption, which fails to pursue or even take account of the manifold connections between his work and aspects of the European modernism which has been available as an alternative tradition, a resource and a referent for continuing experiment and development, throughout the literary history at least of the last sixty years. Pinter himself makes clear the potential importance of this modernist context when he remarks of his early literary tastes and possible influences on his work: 'I was reading . . . a great deal of modern literature, mostly novels . . . I read Hemingway, Dostoevski, Joyce, and Henry Miller at an early age, and Kafka.'[2] Although a connection between Pinter and Kafka has often been noticed, it has rarely been elaborated in sufficient detail to do much more than suggest that the work of each author shares a similar atmosphere of mysterious menace. It is rarer still to find critical discussion of Pinter's work which assesses the possible influence of the other authors he mentions, even when this is apparently at its clearest. The similarity of Pinter's work to Kafka's is hardly more obvious than the resemblance of his drama to the work of the author whom he places at the head of his list of early reading, Ernest

29

Hemingway. Pinter's early plays, in particular, sometimes strongly recall some of Hemingway's early short stories; perhaps Goldberg and McCann in *The Birthday Party*, and certainly Gus and Ben in *The Dumb Waiter*, are clearly comparable to Hemingway's sinister criminals in 'The Killers'. Like Gus and Ben, Hemingway's Al and Max are hired gunmen, uneasily waiting in a restaurant for the arrival of a victim whom they have never met but expect to murder according to instructions. This resemblance in their situations is extended by the language and dialogue of each set of characters. Al and Max are said to look 'like a vaudeville team',[3] and there is a routine, patter-like vacuity in their repetitious exchanges which strongly anticipates the vapid, perfunctory quality which appears in some of Pinter's speeches in *The Dumb Waiter* and more widely in his drama as a whole:

> 'What's yours?' George asked them.
> 'I don't know,' one of the men said. 'What do you want to eat, Al?'
> 'I don't know,' said Al. 'I don't know what I want to eat.'[4]

Like Ben in *The Dumb Waiter*, Al is ironically anxious that his partner talks too much; in fact, the ineffectual reiterations in the terse, spiritless speeches between Hemingway's characters, and in Pinter's play, are remarkable for the paucity of their direct communication.

In another form, the resulting gap between what is actually said and what is communicated provides similar problems for both sets of characters. Both Gus and Ben and Al and Max are disconcertingly confronted, in a comparable manner, by apparent aberrations in the representative function of language: enforced dissociations of words from their referents in the real world. Al's determination to master the other people in the lunch room and keep events wholly under his control is partly thwarted when he finds himself betrayed by a vacuous language. He commits himself to the elaborate, slightly grandiose requests, first of all for 'a roast pork tenderloin with apple sauce and mashed potatoes' and then for 'chicken croquettes with green peas and cream sauce and mashed potatoes',[4] only to be told that neither dish really exists, each belonging to a different menu from the one available. Gus and

Ben are similarly troubled to discover their control of events interrrupted by a dumb waiter which makes culinary demands in increasingly grandiose and elaborate terms whose sophistication they are wholly unable to match in reality. The order for 'Macaroni Pastitsio. Ormitha Macarounada', for example, can only be fulfilled by 'Three McVitie and Price! One Lyons Red Label! One Smith's Crisps! One Eccles Cake! One Fruit and Nut!' (I. 152).[5]

This sort of gap the killers discover between language and reality, a disjuncture between their real situation and the words they encounter and are obliged to use, reappears more widely both in Pinter's drama and in Hemingway's fiction. For example, Gus and Ben's famously extended dispute, occupying two printed pages, about whether the proper instruction is 'light the kettle' or 'light the gas', is only superficially concerned with its ostensible subject, correct usage, and much more profoundly implicated in uneasy developments in relations between the characters, engaged in a power struggle whose existence Ben indicates by asking apparently irrelevantly in the middle of the kettle dispute, 'Who's the senior partner here, me or you?' (I. 142). This sort of exploitation of an uncertain linguistic surface as a context for the conduct of much more deep-rooted psychological conflicts similarly features in Hemingway's fiction. The argument about the kettle, for example, rather resembles events not so much in 'The Killers' as in another early Hemingway piece, also written largely in the form of dialogue, 'Hills Like White Elephants'. In this short story, the man's prosaic refusal to accept his girlfriend's fancifully metaphoric suggestion that 'The hills across the valley of the Ebro . . . "look like white elephants" '[6] is only a superficial aspect and indication of a more profound though unstated refusal to accept her pregnancy. His whole conversation is obliquely directed towards mastering and manoeuvring her into agreeing to an abortion, though this is never mentioned by name in the story. Significantly, the girl's eventual response to the overwhelming duplicity and euphemism in their dialogue is ' "Can't we maybe stop talking? . . . Would you please please please please please please please stop talking?" '[7] This sort of attempted refuge in silence—a final evasive tactic to escape the conversational manipulations of an interlocutor, or an acknowledgement of defeat by them—along with Hemingway's creation of a dialogue idiom in which characters struggle over subjects indirectly defined by their very avoidance of them, directly anticipate the sort of complexities in language and conversation which appear so extensively in Pinter's drama. Pinter himself usefully summarizes some of their nature in his lecture 'Writing for the Theatre' when he discusses

> A language . . . where under what is said, another thing is being said. . . .
> The speech we hear is an indication of that which we don't hear. It is a necessary avoidance, a violent, sly, anguished or mocking smoke screen which keeps the other in its place. . . .
> I think that we communicate only too well, in our silence, in what is unsaid.[8]

The sense of a potential for disjuncture between language and actuality, examined in stories such as 'Hills Like White Elephants' and elsewhere in his fiction, may have been absorbed by Hemingway as one of the disturbing lessons of the First World War. His narrator in *A Farewell to Arms* remarks of wartime experience

> I was always embarassed by the words sacred, glorious, and sacrifice. . . . I had seen nothing sacred, and the things that were glorious had no glory and the sacrifices were like the stockyards at Chicago if nothing was done with the meat except to bury it. There were many words that you could not stand to hear . . . Abstract words such as glory, honour, courage, or hallow were obscene.[9]

Whatever their origins, the sort of anxieties expressed in this passage were widely shared by Hemingway's modernist contemporaries, likewise concerned with the failure of words to connect with the world, and with a referential instability in language which allows it to be used to manipulate and distort rather than represent actuality. Virginia Woolf, for example, in *To the Lighthouse,* has Lily Briscoe suggest that language has somehow fallen out of phase with experience: 'words . . . broke up the thought and dismembered it . . . one could say nothing to nobody. . . . Words fluttered sideways and struck the object inches too low.'[10] The most developed consciousness of language and of the manifold complexities and authorial opportunities extant in its relation to the world is of course to be found in the work of the greatest of modernist novelists, in James Joyce's vast range of styles and parodies in *Ulysses,* and in the linguistic experimentation of *Finnegans Wake.* Like Hemingway, Joyce figures in Pinter's list of early literary tastes, and William Baker and Stephen Ely Tabachnik have shown how thoroughly Pinter was immersed in Joyce's work at an early age. By 16 he was 'deep into' *Finnegans Wake,* having already digested *A Portrait of the Artist as a Young Man* and *Ulysses,* remarking of the latter in a school magazine article that it 'stands supreme among twentieth-century literature. . . . Joyce has always had great feeling for words. . . . no modern writer has used them to such effect.'[11] Joyce's 'great feeling for words'—the sort of feeling that makes the linguistic medium of *Finnegans Wake* as much a subject of the novel as any story it can be found to sustain—is also shared by Pinter, who admits to a 'strong feeling about words'[12] and certainly uses them to better and more subtle effect than any other contemporary British dramatist. It is also shared by some of Pinter's characters, almost more interested in words for what they are than for what they signify. Stanley's relished pronouncement of 'succulent' in *The Birthday Party,* for example, actually obscures its meaning for Meg, while Deeley, in *Old Times,* interrupts what Anna is saying to reflect on her unusual choice of the terms 'lest' and 'gaze' (I. 27; IV. 15, 22).

A related feature which appears more generally in Pinter's work—his creation of a language which functions partly independently of its referential, semantic quality—may also be seen as a legacy of his admiration for Joyce. Both the linguistic autonomy of *Finnegans Wake* and the parodies which feature so extensively in *Ulysses* illustrate the possibility that the manner and style of an utterance can be as significant, and as communicative, as any primary referential function of the words spoken. Ruth, in *The Homecoming,* suggests an extreme version of this sort of possibility when she remarks

> My lips move. Why don't you restrict . . . your observations to that? Perhaps the fact that they move is more significant . . . than the words which come through them. You must bear that . . . possibility . . . in mind. (III. 69)

This 'possibility', that language signifies not only directly but obliquely through its particular nature, or through the manner or context of its utterance, is one whose importance for an understanding of Pinter's work several critics have observed. John Russell Brown, for example, in *Theatre Language*, suggests of one Pinter episode

> If only the sounds of the words were heard, or if the dialogue was followed by someone not knowing a word of English, much of the pressures, tactics and moments of decision . . . would be communicated.[13]

Though Brown's suggestion could not be extended into a thoroughgoing conclusion about Pinter, in whose work the significance of primary meaning certainly does not wholly disappear, it is nevertheless clear that like one of his characters, he has 'often wondered what "mean" means' (III. 115), presenting and examining in his drama a full range of communicative possibilities, indirect as well as direct, which develop and illustrate the complexity of characters' inter-relations and attempts to influence each other not only through what is said but through the manner of saying it. Manner and style are often much more significant than meaning in *The Birthday Party*, for example when Goldberg and McCann batter Stanley with questions which are almost entirely rhetorical. Merciless and incomprehensible, their interrogation seeks not information but the intimidation of their victim. This intention is certainly 'more significant than the words', as Stanley realizes when he translates their verbal aggression into a reply of physical violence.

Goldberg and McCann's sinister catechism is only one example of Pinter's frequent deployment of 'A language . . . where under what is said, another thing is being said.' Austin Quigley, an intelligent commentator on this aspect of Pinter's work, summarizes the problem it presents by suggesting

> language is primarily used in the negotiation of the relationship[s] . . . rather than for its overall referential possibilities. . . . As long as criticism is handicapped by an implicit belief that language is primarily referential, that it is mainly concerned with the transfer of verifiable facts, we will continue to be puzzled.[14]

34

Some of this puzzlement has already been dispelled by critics such as Quigley, sensitive to Pinter's linguistic complexity, though this most distinctive feature of Pinter's style can be further clarified if his exploration and exploitation of the potential disjuncture between language and the world it ought to represent is more widely recognized as having originated among the sort of modernist authors, Hemingway and Joyce particularly, whose work first appealed to Pinter's imagination and formed his early literary experience. As Guido Almansi and Simon Henderson suggest in a recent study, 'For [Pinter], as for the post-modernist world generally, it is *language* that provides the supreme obstacle.'[15] This obstacle and its nature are better understood if Pinter's ingenious theatre language is appreciated as a feature of 'the post-modernist world', and if Pinter's work is recognized not as a radically unusual departure from tradition, but as part of a wider movement and concern with language affecting much of twentieth-century literature. The obvious resemblance between the problems of Hemingway's killers and Pinter's is thus not of only incidental interest, but provides a convenient introduction to a much wider set of affinities which help place and clarify Pinter's work in the context of modern literary history.

The binary function of 'a language . . . where under what is said, another thing is being said' is only part of a further duality, a mixture of an objective, realistic surface with a more subjective, psychological substratum, which is characteristic of Pinter's drama as a whole, and also worth considering in the light of his reading of earlier fiction. The ostentatious, careful realism of speech and setting is a strong enough feature of his plays to have misled early critics into including his work in the 'kitchen sink' school of drama which appeared in the '50s. But such verisimilitude, seeming to locate the plays firmly in the ordinary, everyday world, is only superficial, partly a distraction from the mainspring of Pinter's dramatic action: a 'sly, anguished or mocking smoke screen' for the central concern of his plays with the working out of characters' covert psychological compulsions. Pinter himself suggests this sort of duality when he remarks 'what goes on in my plays is realistic, but what I'm doing is not realism.'[16] Sometimes the division in his drama between a plausibly realistic, objective surface and a more subjective level of psychological concern is elucidated by a clear bifurcation in a play's structure; *The Lover,* for example, shows a suburban couple who lead a normal enough life in mornings and evenings, while indulging in an elaborate series of sexual fantasies in the afternoons. Such a precise and sustained separation of the everyday domain from the subjective, psychological one is rare, however; more often such separation is brief and local, as in *The Birthday Party,* for example, where the division between Stanley's public persona and his private ennervation is signified by the way his apparently self-confident speech 'Tell me Mrs. Boles, when you address yourself to me, do you ever ask yourself who exactly you are talking to?' is immediately succeeded by the stage direction 'Silence. He groans, his trunk falls forward, his head falls into his hands' (I. 31). Even clues such as these are rare, however. In fact, it is the peculiarly pervasive intermingling of ordinary, humdrum daily life with the realms of fantasy or psychological rather than surface reality which contributes the disturbingly mystifying quality to Pinter's drama.

One of his earliest critics, writing in *The Times* in 1960, immediately identified the connection of this feature of his writing with modernist fiction by describing it as 'Kafkaesque mystery'.[17] Recorded as part of Pinter's list of early reading, Kafka's fiction offers several illuminating analogies with Pinter's work. One of his earliest pieces of writing, 'The Examination', has a distinctly Kafka quality, and even has a 'K.' figure, Kullus, as one of its characters. And Pinter's first play, *The Room,* resembles Kafka not only generally in creating a roughly similar atmosphere of uneasiness and intangible menace, but quite specifically in developing a sense of external threat in terms comparable to Kafka's in his short stories, especially 'The Burrow'. Kafka's insecure burrowing creature, whose uneasy monologue provides the substance of this story, precisely shares the sort of anxieties from which many of Pinter's characters suffer:

> in reality, the burrow does provide a considerable degree of security, but by no means enough, for is one ever free from anxieties inside it? . . . simply by virtue of being owner of this great vulnerable edifice I am obviously defenceless against any serious attack.[18]

'The Burrow' provides almost a parable version of feelings in several Pinter plays, some of which are aptly summarized by Rose in *The Room:*

> This is a good room. You've got a chance in a place like this. . . . you can move yourself, you can come home at night, if you have to go out, you can do your job, you can come home, you're all right. . . . You stand a chance. (I. 105)

Like Kafka's creature, however, Rose finds her eagerness to confine herself to the security of her lair qualified by a fearful fascination with the outside world and its menaces, an intense curiosity about the house which contains her room, for example. This building seems peculiarly worthy of her interest. When asked how many floors it contains, the landlord replies 'Well, to tell you the truth, I don't count them now' (I. 108); the building seems as intricate and undefinably extended as the Emperor's Palace in another Kafka short story, 'The Great Wall of China'.

Pinter himself summarizes the theme of *The Room* in remarking 'A man in a room and no one entering lives in expectation of a visit. . . . But however much it is expected the entrance, when it comes, is unexpected and almost always unwelcome.'[19] Though such concerns, defined in his first play, reappear throughout his drama, and can be specifically retraced to a Kafka story, a still more general resemblance between the two authors arises from Pinter's habitual combination of a humdrum naturalistic surface with a darker, psychologically-motivated action: the sort of 'friction of nightmare and normality',[20] as J. L. Styan calls it, whose appearance in Pinter's work is outlined above. As Edwin Muir was first to recognize, the peculiar quality of Kafka's writing likewise results not—or not only—from his talent for projecting anxieties and psychic disturbances into strange, hallucinatory realizations, but from a careful grounding of these fantastic projections in a faithfully detailed attentiveness to the mundane and everyday. Thus one of Gregor Samsa's first thoughts on awakening to find himself transformed into a gigantic insect does not concern the monstrosity of his metamorphosis, but simply the irritating likelihood that because of 'his dome-like belly . . . the bed-quilt could hardly keep in position and was about to slide off completely'.[21] Like this banal anxiety about the bed-clothes, the pervasive and meticulous inclusion of quotidien detail—cornflakes, fried bread, and all—in Pinter's *The Birthday Party*, for example, provides a strangely compelling contextualization for the more bizarre developments involved: a disturbingly convincing location for an action best explained, if explicable at all, not in terms of the everyday world in which the play is set, but as a projection into that world of the psychological processes of its protagonist, Stanley. Just as the polite, well-dressed pair who remove Joseph K. for execution at the end of Kafka's *The Trial* cannot be rationalized as members of any police or terrorist force operational in the actual world, but as partly dream-realizations, images of the protagonist's uneasy psyche, so the action of figures such as Goldberg and McCann, incomprehensible in naturalistic terms, is much more easily understood if they are seen partly as realizations, images, arising from Stanley's guilty sense of torpid inadequacy. It is significant how directly the fantasy that 'They're coming in a van . . . looking for someone . . . a certain person' (I. 34), which Stanley uses to frighten Meg, prefigures his own fate; Goldberg and McCann, or figures like them, are, literally, in Stanley's mind before they appear on stage.

Part of the fascination of Pinter's drama is that like Kafka's fiction, some of its mysteriousness cannot be wholly explained. However, early critics who concluded on the other hand that Pinter's plays were wholly incomprehensible simply failed to look beyond their naturalistic surface. Whatever the ultimate elusiveness of Pinter's drama, it cannot be either entirely or gratuitously mystifying, or audiences would not feel the compulsion to return to it which the continuing success of the plays clearly indicates. This compelling quality may result partly from the very deficiencies in apparent logic in the naturalistic surfaces of Pinter's plays, which encourage audiences at least to intuit, if not necessarily to rationalize immediately, some impulse originating in the psyches of the characters involved, behind this bewildering surface. Whether or not Pinter actually learned from Kafka his strategy of creating this compelling amalgam of realism and the noumenal dream-domain, it is a definite advantage to keep the example of Kafka in mind when encountering Pinter's work. Though Kafka remains as challenging a writer as ever, his characteristic difficulties have at least grown familiar and comprehensible in ways which can be usefully extended through analogy to an examination of similar perplexities in Pinter's work.

Aspects of Pinter's simultaneous vision of reality and of the subjective domain of his characters may be further elucidated by more general comparison with some of the techniques of modernist fiction. One of the most useful insights into the nature of Pinter's dramatic action is offered by the author himself when he remarks of *The Caretaker:* 'the one thing that people have missed is that it isn't necessary to conclude that everything Aston says about his experiences in the mental hospital is true.'[22] This suggestion of his characters' possible mendacity is obviously helpful at one level in removing the need for critics to tie themselves in interpretive knots over problems such as whether Stanley is really a concert pianist who once performed in the unlikely location of Lower Edmonton, and may do so again in 'Constantinople. Zagreb. Vladivostok'. (I. 32); or whether Solto, in *Night School*, really killed 'a six foot ten lascar from Madagascar' (II. 213). Such impressive-sounding claims are most plausibly understood as further aspects of characters' exploitation of a language disjunct from reality as part of their strategies of power, manipulation or self-protection. At another level, however, Pinter's apparently helpful admission that his dramas may break the stage convention that characters always tell the truth about themselves (or at least allow the audience a clear indication of when they fail to do so) actually contributes to a more general interpretive problem of his plays, their paucity of reliable exposition. Whereas most dramatic characters have sufficient to say for themselves (and sufficiently truthful things to say) to allow an audience to reconstruct almost effortlessly a plausible identity for them, Pinter's characters are much less clearly and much less reliably self-revealing. Pinter himself defends this feature of his drama by suggesting

> a character on the stage who can present no convincing argument or information as to his past experience, his present

39

behaviour or his aspirations, nor give a comprehensive analysis of his motives is as legitimate and as worthy of attention as one who, alarmingly, can do all these things.[23]

In addition to this defence, it might be argued that the whole action of some Pinter plays can be seen as expositional; rather than developing as in conventional drama, Pinter characters sometimes only elucidate continuing psychic states or uneasy equilibria, of the sort which seems to exist between Duff and Beth in *Landscape,* for example. Nevertheless, Pinter's excision of most conventional dramatic exposition, and his making unreliable of the self-definition of characters such as Aston, imposes new demands on the deductive powers of an audience, forced to assess character and action on the basis of clues whose validity it largely has to establish for itself.

Such new demands are interestingly analogous to those initially made on its readership by modernist fiction, one of whose distinctive qualities is its involvement of the reader in the creation or re-creation of a fictional world often presented through the narration or transcribed consciousness of a potentially unreliable character, rather than wholly directly or definitively presented by the author. This sort of fiction Roland Barthes defines as '*scriptible*' in distinction to the '*lisible*' nineteenth-century fictional idiom, predominantly realist, in which a conveniently omniscient, objective author presents his fictional world fully and reliably and without obliging the reader to verify the reliability of the narrative. So bereft of conventional exposition, Pinter's dramatic strategy clearly corresponds to Barthes' view of the '*scriptible*' aspect of modern writing; audiences have to involve themselves in the attempt to fathom a world not wholly or immediately clarified for them, and made more perplexing by Pinter's partial adoption, in the manner discussed above in connection with *The Birthday Party,* of one of the most characteristic devices of modernist fiction, the interpolation of a character's consciousness between audience and fictional world. Unused to the possibility that the action presented and some of the past events mentioned may be partly projections of a character's consciousness, the early television audience of *The Basement,* for example, as Martin Esslin records, were simply 'disconcerted by the difficulty of deciding whether the action was real or imagined'.[24] Pinter himself may first have been impressed by the 'disconcerting' tactic of presenting a world partly refracted through the consciousness of one of the characters in it by his reading of '*scriptible*' novels; at any rate, as with other aspects of his drama, this strategy is less 'difficult' if it is considered in the context of the more familiar innovations of the modernist novel.

This context is relevant not only to the distinctive use of language, the intermingling of subjective and objective visions and the general challenge to interpretation which are distinctive features of Pinter's early drama, and originally made it seem so challengingly innovative. His later plays show a concern with what Edward in *A Slight Ache* might define as 'the dimensionality and continuity of space . . . and time' (I. 177), and this concern bears extensive comparison with an interest among modernist novelists in the nature of time and in the formal possibilities offered by amendment of the temporal dimension of their fiction. Several modernist writers' concentration on the subjective consciousness of their characters extends to an incorporation of their past histories into the texture of the fiction by means of those characters' memories; recollections of earlier times which occur to Bloom, or to Mrs. Dalloway, for example, are used to incorporate an extensive sense of their past lives into the narration of the single days which occupy *Ulysses* and *Mrs. Dalloway*. Such an interest in memory and its use as a narrative device is probably most developed in Marcel Proust's *À la Recherche du Temps Perdu*, which Pinter adapted into *The Proust Screenplay* in 1972, remarking that 'the subject was Time . . . Working on *À la Recherche du Temps Perdu* was the best working year of my life.'[25] Though Pinter's interest in time and memory seems to have intensified in the plays written since his discovery, or rediscovery, of Proust, it is also discernible before 1972, and may originally have been part of a more general legacy of modernist fiction. Pinter ponders in 1962, for example,

> We are faced with the immense difficulty, if not the impossibility, of verifying the past. I don't mean merely years ago, but yesterday, this morning. What took place, what was the nature of what took place, what happened?[26]

41

Though such concerns seem most directly shared by Hirst—who remarks of the past in *No Man's Land* (1974) 'It's gone. Did it exist? It's gone. It never existed. It remains.' (IV. 108)—they also appear in *Old Times* (1970). One of the characters, Anna, sums up the blend in this play of fact with memory, of present consciousness with 'old times', when she remarks: 'There are some things one remembers even though they may never have happened. There are things I remember which may never have happened but as I recall them so they take place' (IV. 27–8). As Anna's remarks help to suggest, *Old Times* follows Pinter's earlier plays in presenting events warped by the consciousness of the characters involved, though this consciousness is now substantially focused upon memories, recollections of the past, and imaginings about old lost times. In one of his most recent plays, *Betrayal*, Pinter makes this retrospective imperative even more palpable, using it as the structural basis for the play, which comprises nine scenes set largely in inverse order at various stages of the betraying affair, beginning at 1977, and tracing it back to its inception in 1968.

Pinter's drama, then, shows a manifold set of connections—concerned with language, subjectivity, narrative difficulty, time and memory—with the sort of modernist fiction which he identifies as his earliest reading and resumed in studying Proust in the '70s. Such suggestive connections inevitably raise the question of influence and imitation; as George Wellwarth remarks of Pinter's drama, 'His works . . . remind one of other works in an allusive manner—in a manner, that is to say, as if Pinter had been unconsciously influenced by something he had read.'[27] Pinter himself admits 'You don't write in a vacuum: you're bound to absorb and digest other writing',[28] and it is not surprising that the work he read and admired at an early and formative stage in his imaginative development—Joyce while still at school—later contributes to some of the concerns which appear in his drama, and may have affected the choice of forms and styles through which these are presented. As Wellwarth suggests, any such contribution probably takes place at the level of unconscious influence. It is neither necessary nor helpful to suggest any more direct learning or borrowing by Pinter from modernism; probably only in *The Dumb Waiter* does he come anywhere near a more straightforward, undifferentiated adoption of a situation he might have found in earlier writing. Pinter has in any case shown himself sensibly wary of suggestions of 'undigested' assimilation of the work of earlier authors; of his possible debts to Beckett and to Kafka he has at various times remarked 'I'm not sure what influence means in this connexion' and 'when I read them it rang a bell, that's all, within me. I thought: something is going on here which is going on in me too.'[29] This latter suggestion is helpfully indicative both of a proper means of connecting Pinter to earlier authors, and of a critical approach to his work so far too rarely explored. Discussion of Pinter in relation to possible antecedents need not conclude in terms of direct imitation, nor with the rather vague generalizations employed by James R. Hollis, for example, in suggesting 'The mysterious authority of Goldberg and McCann over Stanley should not be a surprise to those who have stood the watch with K before the castle.'[30] Pinter criticism requires to go further than Hollis does, proceeding from analogy to analysis. Whatever the nature and origins of Pinter's affinities with earlier literature, once it has been recognized that some of the things 'going on' in the modernist idiom are also 'going on' in his drama, the critical familiarity developed over the past fifty years with modernism and its techniques can be brought to bear to assist an understanding of some of the perplexities that Pinter has undoubtedly presented over the past twenty-five. Much of the puzzling quality of Pinter's work can be dispelled, or at least placed in context, by such analytic comparison of his visions of language, time, and subjectivity, and of the techniques and devices he creates for their presentation, with those of modernist novelists before him. Such comparison also suggests that the radical originality often attributed to Pinter as an explanation of his apparent oddities is in one sense only a distraction from proper appreciation of his true status as an author who has extended into new areas and recent decades many of the challenging structural and ideological innovations which distinguish the modernist novel.

*   *   *

Paradoxically, such a dismissal of Pinter's claims to originality only serves to highlight their actual validity, albeit in different terms from those usually assumed. A genuinely original aspect of Pinter's work is his extension onto the stage of innovations which had previously been almost exclusively the property of fiction. It is significant in this respect that Pinter's list of early reading, quoted at the start of the present essay, was proffered in an interview as part of an emphatic denial of any influence from the experimental drama written earlier in the century by such authors as Brecht and Pirandello. Pinter also records elsewhere: 'I saw very few plays . . . before I was twenty.'[31] To some extent, his connection with fictional rather than dramatic antecedents is natural; Pinter began his literary career as a short story writer, and his transference to the dramatic idiom is in some ways a surprising achievement, as, objectively viewed, many of the interests which later emerge in his plays seem more suitable for fiction rather than realization on stage. (Incidentally, this may perhaps explain why Pinter has so far had very few successful imitators in the theatre.) For example, involvement of the reader in the psyche of a single individual, around whom strange or fantastic psychic figurations may be projected, seems a much easier achievement for the novel, where a simple restriction of point of view is sufficient to effect the necessary concentration on individual consciousness, as the modernist novel often demonstrates. Despite the possible example of Strindberg's *A Dream Play*, or of some of Pirandello's work, this sort of concentration is obviously more difficult to achieve on stage, where it may seem impossible to make the audience share the point of view of a single character, and inevitable that all figures presented, Goldberg and McCann as much as Stanley, for example, share the same palpable reality as creatures of flesh and blood rather than projections of psyche or imagination. Perhaps it is significant that Pinter, more than most contemporary English dramatists, has turned to radio and television for the staging of his plays. Television in particular, like the novel, can achieve the restriction of point of view to an individual character's troubled consciousness. Pinter exploits this possibility to good effect in *The Basement*, for example, and in representing Disson's double vision in *Tea Party*, in which the stage direction

44

'Disson's point of view' appears increasingly often as the play progresses and narrows its focus on his deteriorating stability. Similarly, radio drama offers the possibility of leaving open any questions about the real or imaginary status of characters, as Pinter successfully illustrates in the mysterious figure of the matchseller in *A Slight Ache*.

Nevertheless, the success of Pinter's drama in the theatre, as well as on radio and television, testifies to the possibility of discovering means for realizing similar effects on stage. A distinction of singular points of view is clearly enough achieved in *Landscape*, for example, by the radical disjuncture in the testimonies of Duff and Beth. It is a peculiarity of the English stage in the twentieth century, however, that when Pinter first came to write for it in 1957, he was obliged to work out any such innovative techniques almost entirely for himself, as earlier English theatrical history offered him so little in the way of models or antecedents for his need to experiment. The revolution in styles and structures of fiction and of poetry wrought by modernism in the early decades of the century was not matched by much similar experimentation or innovation in English drama, which remained on the whole distinctly conservative not only between the wars but almost until the time Pinter's work first appeared. As J. B. Priestley, one of the more popular dramatists of the time, remarked in 1939

> it happens that our London Theatre is about the least experimental in the world, and is always badly in need of a production that is not exactly like all the last two hundred-and-one productions. We have great theatrical activity in our capital . . . but it is mostly activity of a kind that the intelligent foreign visitor finds it more polite to ignore.[32]

Perhaps the conservatism Priestley identifies can be partly explained by the predominance among contemporary audiences of the middle class, no doubt content to see their own milieu and preoccupations presented time after 201st time within the box sets, usually depicting the drawing room of a well-to-do family, which appeared so frequently on the English stage of the period. Changing circumstances among this class between the wars perhaps heightened such self-interest. Diminished prosperity following the depredations of the First

World War, and especially in the '30s, imperilled financial security in a way that could be examined in somewhat Chekhovian, elegiac dramas reflecting this partial decline. Two of J. B. Priestley's own popular '30s plays, *Time and the Conways* and *An Inspector Calls*, for example, are fairly directly concerned to chart the bankruptcy of the middle class in, respectively, financial and moral terms. Priestley's dramas also recurrently show an intense nostalgia for the securer days before the First World War, sometimes actually incorporated into the structure of his plays as part of his interest in fourth-dimensional theories of time.

Whatever changes had occurred in reality since 1914, these remained largely unmatched by stylistic or formal developments on the stage. Priestley's 'intelligent foreign visitor', acquainted with the innovations in European dramatic technique in the early twentieth century wrought by the work of Strindberg, Pirandello, German Expressionism, Brecht, and others, might have been legitimately puzzled to discover the continuing predominance on the London stage of the sort of bourgeois naturalism that had been partly ousted from the Continental theatre since the end of the nineteenth century. Such formal conservatism, aptly described by Priestley as 'lacking in originality and vitality',[33] was not, however, wholly unchallenged by attempts to amend or overthrow naturalistic convention. Although apparently largely conventional and naturalistic, some of Priestley's own successful '30s plays are also subtly marked by what he calls 'drifting away from naturalism . . . [and] the flavourless patter of modern realistic English dialogue'.[34] Some inclination towards experimentation with an expressionist idiom is already evident, for example, in the demand of the stage directions in *An Inspector Calls* for particular lighting effects to create an unreal, ghostly ambience for the unearthly figure of Inspector Goole. This 'drifting away from naturalism', and the need to find what Priestley calls 'a suitable framework for my "timeless" method', culminate in *Johnson Over Jordan*, described by its author as 'a dream play— though . . . not what Strindberg was after in his dream plays'.[35] Priestley's further explanation that the play attempts to create 'a prolonged dream-like state . . . filled with hallucinatory visions directly resultant from the mental-content of the percipient'[36] helps to suggest that *Johnson Over Jordan* may be seen as a rare example of an earlier English drama which bears comparison with Pinter's concern with the 'mental content' of characters and his projection of this 'dream-like . . . hallucinatory' material in stage terms. As Ronald Hayman has suggested,[37] the figures of the First and Second Examiners, Kafkaesque differentiations of Johnson's own guilt and anxiety, are particularly comparable to Goldberg and McCann, especially in their penchant for threatening interrogative irrelevancy—variously demanding of Jordan, for example:

> You are a husband—and a father? . . . is your best good enough? . . . How far have you tried to acquaint yourself with the findings of chemistry, physics, biology, geology, astronomy, mathematics?[38]

Another and more substantial antecedent for Pinter's developments may be found in the work of T. S. Eliot, another of the rare figures who contemplated the reformation of English drama in the '30s. Eliot's particular ambition, to reintroduce poetry to the stage, was partly a correlative of his need for a heightened idiom in which to present dramas of spiritual initiation and expiation, concerned, not unlike Priestley's *Johnson Over Jordan*, with the souls of their protagonists. This mood of spiritual enquiry was not incongruous in the ecclesiastical setting of *Murder in the Cathedral*, whose remote historical period also helped its audience to accept and naturalize the action. Eliot, however, did not feel that this success was the achievement he sought, remarking that he wanted a closer 'contact with the ordinary everyday world'[39] in his drama. Significantly, he seems to have assumed that 'the ordinary everyday world' in theatrical terms meant the sort of box set and upper middle-class family milieu which so dominated the stage at the time, and turned to this setting in his next play *The Family Reunion*, despite its distinctly undomestic themes of Oresteian guilt, mystic insight and spiritual freedom. The result is a peculiar play whose rather static, visible action in the naturalistic drawing-room context almost wholly masks its significant psychological action. This concerns Harry's liberation from the accursed confusions of his family and his own guilty obsessions, partly achieved by the revelation of the true parental circumstances preceding his birth. Superficially concerned with Lady Amy Monchesney's birthday celebrations, and ending with a sort of rebirth for Harry and a ritual dance around a birthday cake, the play might almost have been called *The Birthday Party*, and its theme of release from spiritual atrophy and torpor bears some comparison with Pinter's play.

Pinter's affinities with Eliot, however, are more formal than thematic. Early audiences were somewhat bewildered by Eliot's plays, as they were by Pinter's, and perhaps for the similar reason that in each case they were unable to disentangle the play's significant psychological action from a distracting, masking, naturalistic surface. Several characters in Eliot's plays usefully define this aspect of dramatic structure. It is remarked in *The Family Reunion*, for example: 'Everything is true in a different sense. . . . In this world/ It is inexplicable, the resolution is in another.' Sir Henry Harcourt-Reilly quotes Zoroaster to explain the similarly mysterious action of *The Cocktail Party*: 'know there are two worlds of life and death:/ One that which thou beholdest; but the other/ Is underneath the grave.'[40] Such a summary indication of the duality in Eliot's drama, and of the existence of 'two worlds . . . one that which thou beholdest . . . the other is underneath', also aptly suggests Pinter's Kafkaesque interfusion of superficial naturalism in an action whose logic and motives originate not in the everyday world portrayed but in the psyches of its inhabitants.

Possibly in some of Priestley's work, then, certainly in T. S. Eliot's drama, and perhaps in the plays of other contemporary experimenters in verse drama (such as W. H. Auden and Christopher Fry), Pinter might have found some earlier examples of the sort of innovations he introduced to the stage in the '50s, and not only in the formal and thematic terms outlined above, but also in some of these playwrights' use of language. The witty, stycomythic interchanges of Eliot's early fragment, *Sweeney Agonistes*, for example, as well as its unsettling atmosphere, might be traced into Pinter's plays. Such possible models for Pinter in earlier English drama are few, however, and made more unpromising by the dubious reception they had received when they first appeared. Attempts at experiment in the English theatre in the early twentieth century are on the whole more instructive about the contemporary strength of convention they encountered than they were successful in diminishing it at the time. Priestley records of the equivocal reception of *Johnson Over Jordan*, for example:

> a hostile or stupid press badly damaged [the] play's chances. Nor did we ever succeed in capturing the interest of the well-to-do play-going public. . . . the fate of this play left me more firmly convinced than ever that our whole method of serious theatrical presentation in this country will have to be changed or very soon there will not be left us even a glimmer of dramatic art.[41]

Some of the changes which Priestley may have been hoping for in methods of theatrical presentation, and, concomitantly, perhaps even in the composition of the play-going public, did eventually begin to appear just in time for Pinter's debut in 1957. It is now a critical cliché that, as Hollis expresses it,

> Nothing much besides the verse drama of Eliot and Fry and the usual commercial froth had come out of England since World War II until that May of 1956 when John Osborne's *Look Back in Anger* exploded and changed the course of English Theatre.[42]

A truer picture is presented by acknowledging that the course of English drama was changed in the mid-'50s not only by Osborne, but by the Absurdist, philosophical theatre of Samuel Beckett, and perhaps also by Eugene Ionesco; *Waiting for Godot* was first performed in London in 1955, and Ionesco's *The Bald Prima Donna* in 1956. Puzzled reviewers of *The Birthday Party*, first produced in 1958, were quick to turn to Absurd drama as a possible source of Pinter's oddity, suggesting that 'This essay in surrealist drama . . . gives the impression of deriving from a Ionesco play which M. Ionesco has not yet written', and that 'Harold Pinter's first play comes in the school of random dottiness deriving from Beckett and Ionesco and before the flourishing continuance of which one quails in slack-jawed dismay.'[43] Pinter himself claimed in 1967 'I'd never heard of Ionesco until after I'd written the first few plays', oddly obscuring his earlier admission in *The Times* in 1959 that 'when I wrote *The Birthday Party* I had . . . seen one of his plays, *The New Tenant*.'[44] This Ionesco play, performed in London in November 1956, actually shows some quite close affinities with Pinter's first play, *The Room* (May 1957). Ionesco's *Caretaker* is moved to vacuous but increasingly inventive torrents of language when confronted by the insouciantly masterful silence of the Gentleman, rather as Rose is in relation to Bert in *The Room*; while the mysterious determination of this Gentleman to immure himself completely, blocking off windows and doors with monumental piles of furniture, bears some analogy with the urge for refuge in a secure 'burrow' shared by several of Pinter's characters, Rose included.

The ostentatiousness with which Ionesco's drama eschews even apparent verisimilitude of action, however, distinguishes his work from Pinter's. Analogy of the two dramatists seems more of a refuge for puzzled reviewers than an observation which can be usefully extended much beyond the similarities suggested between *The Room* and *The New Tenant*. Pinter's debts to Osborne are probably even more minimal. In any case, the changes Osborne introduced to the English stage seem in retrospect much less 'explosive' than Hollis suggests; far from breaking the predominant naturalism of earlier decades of English theatre, Osborne merely adjusted its social range slightly downwards, and changed the conventional drawing-room box set for a combined sitting room-kitchen in *Look Back in Anger*. The prior appearance of such 'kitchen sink' domestic realism in the work of Osborne and other 'Angry Young Men', however, led some early critics to associate with them the shabby milieux of Pinter's plays, and his meticulous reproduction of a range of speech patterns, including those of the lower classes and of down-and-outs. But since realism, domestic or otherwise, is only superficial aspect of Pinter's drama, such a comparison was something of a false start. An apparently more apt suggestion of a relation between Osborne's work and Pinter's came from Ruby Cohn, who remarks:

> Pinter is not only Beckett's spiritual son. He is at least a cousin of the Angry Young Englishmen of his generation. . . . Like Osborne, Pinter looks back in anger; like Beckett, Pinter looks forward to nothing.[45]

Several other critics shared this idea that Pinter's work was a sort of synthesis of Osborne and his kitchen-sink school with the metaphysical interests and anxieties of dramatists such as

Beckett and Ionesco, and their views interestingly indicate that a duality of focus immediately seemed to early critics to be an important aspect of Pinter's work. Nevertheless, as suggested already, Pinter's mixture of superficial realism with more profound psychological concerns is directly comparable to a quality of Kafka's novels, and more likely to derive from Pinter's early appreciation of them than from any later synthesis of his genuine admiration for Beckett with new developments in naturalist drama which happened to be appearing in the work of Osborne and other 'Angry Young Englishmen' at the time.

Pinter himself has suggested his likely indebtedness to Beckett. He remarks, for example, 'If Beckett's influence shows in my work that's all right with me. . . . I admire Beckett's work so much that something of its texture might appear in my own.'[46] Pinter's admiration for Beckett is most clearly reflected in the 'texture' of the dialogue, and in the general concern with language, which appear in his early plays. The sort of abbreviated, repetitive interchanges which characterize the speeches of Vladimir and Estragon in *Waiting for Godot* reappear in the rapid, minimal communications of Gus and Ben in *The Dumb Waiter*, Goldberg and McCann in *The Birthday Party*, and Mick and Davies in *The Caretaker*. And although Pinter's characters, like Beckett's, find their ability to communicate inhibited by vicissitudes in the nature of words and speech, they also share a similar need and facility for using language as a self-substantive device, an antidote to the silences which surround and threaten them. As well as comparable linguistic interests, the concern with time and memory which is a particular feature of Pinter's later drama is also shared with Beckett; some of the questions about memory, time and the continuity of identity which trouble Krapp in *Krapp's Last Tape* and puzzle Vladimir and Estragon in *Waiting for Godot* similarly affect Pinter's later memory plays, *Old Times* and *Landscape* in particular. In addition to such general concerns with language and time, more specific connections with Beckett's work might also be suggested; Davies, in *The Caretaker*, may appear to be a distant relation of Beckett's tramps in *Waiting for Godot*, and Gus and Ben seem still more direct descendants. From its punning title onwards, *The Dumb Waiter* strongly resembles *Waiting for Godot* in situation as well as dialogue. Like Vladimir and Estragon, Gus and Ben dumbly await a fate which they cannot control or anticipate, yet cannot or may not wish to escape, and are similarly disturbed by messages and intrusions apparently from a world beyond their own, like Vladimir and Estragon confronted by the boy who may have come from Godot. In fact, what Pinter's second play does not derive from Hemingway's 'The Killers', it seems to take largely from Samuel Beckett.

Perhaps it is the obviousness of some of Pinter's affinities with Beckett which has led to their occasional exaggeration by critics, at the expense of other significant connections between his work and earlier literature. To call Pinter 'Beckett's spiritual son', for example, suggests too direct a descent. Though Davies, like Vladimir and Estragon, is a tramp, he could not easily be transposed from Aston's paraphernalia-strewn domain to the altogether vaguer setting of *Waiting for Godot*, a deliberately generalized context for Beckett's more widely-ranging philosophical and metaphysical presentation of the human condition. Vladimir and Estragon simply claim at one stage 'all mankind is us', and describe Pozzo as 'all humanity'[47]; though some of their problems may be shared by 'all mankind', the significance of Pinter's characters is more circumscribed by specific individuation, and in accent and dialect as well as stage setting, they belong more closely— though sometimes still only partially—to a recognizable social world. So for all its obvious similarities, some careful distinction of Pinter's drama from Beckett's is nevertheless worthwhile. It is perhaps also significant that Pinter records being extremely impressed by Beckett's *novels* at an early age, before reading his plays, and that he mentions a particular admiration for Beckett as 'the best prose writer living',[48] rather than only, or primarily, as a dramatist. From Beckett's fiction Pinter may have learned some of his tactics for presenting in detail disturbed or unusual states of mind, and such techniques are probably as important a feature of his drama as anything that may have been absorbed from Beckett's plays. Once again, fiction rather than drama provides the primary antecedent for Pinter's work.

So, to return to the opening question, is Pinter an innovator?

Harold Pinter—Innovator?

Yes, certainly—in terms of his substantially independent creation of a theatrical idiom. Despite some possible connections, of the sort outlined above, of Pinter's drama with developments attempted by authors such as Priestley and Eliot, or with the more decisive changes later introduced to the English stage by Osborne, Ionesco and Beckett, the sum of his indebtedness to earlier dramatists is small, and hardly significantly extended beyond some acknowledged overlaps in texture with Beckett. As suggested at the start of this essay, such originality in specifically theatrical terms requires to be seen in the context of the sort of innovations made by the modernist fiction which formed Pinter's early reading, but although this broader literary perspective indicates that his sort of developments and interests had appeared long before his plays devised dramatic means for their expression, this observation should neither detract from estimation of Pinter's worth, nor too much inhibit admiration of his originality as a writer for the theatre. Even if the most clearly derivative of his plays, *The Dumb Waiter*, is taken as an example, it can be acknowledged that although it is largely a synthesis of earlier developments— quite specifically of 'The Killers' and *Waiting for Godot*—there is an admirable originality in Pinter's recognition of the possibilities of an amalgamation of such material, and in the theatrical ingenuity with which this is achieved.

One of the most characteristic and impressive features of this sort of dramatic ingenuity is the modesty of the scale on which it operates. Pinter himself remarks 'I always think of the normal picture-frame stage which I used as an actor',[49] and his plays have never required the sort of radical amendments in staging which accompanied the appearance of expressionist, Absurdist, or other experimental forms of twentieth-century drama. Instead, Pinter's real achievement has been that while apparently remaining more or less within accepted theatrical decorum—even within the conventional picture-frame stage— he has established a style, pace and dramatic language which allows for the incorporation into the theatre not only of the sort of investigations and projections of individual consciousness which distinguishes the work of Kafka and other contemporary novelists, but also of many of the other strengths of modernism, such as its interests in time, language and memory. In creating the ambivalence of presentation and diminution of objectivity such interests require, he has retained much of the appearance of naturalist theatre while subtly and provocatively altering many of its habits and expectations. In the course of such developments, Pinter has added considerably to the resources of the British stage and of its actors; as an early *Times* review remarked

> *The Birthday Party* is the Ur-text of modern British drama: if John Osborne fired new authors into writing, Pinter showed them how to write. He relieved them of the dead weight of naturalism, and offered a comic idiom that took its starting point from significant language and significant action.[50]

As J. B. Priestley suggests, the stage is an area on which 'it is dangerous in this country to try and advance on any front',[51] and the ingenuity with which Pinter has done so largely merits the sort of critical admiration which Bernard Dukore summarizes in remarking that 'it is commonplace to call Pinter one of the best living dramatists who write in the English language— or in any language.'[52]

A paradox in Pinter's reception, however, is that the extensive critical esteem for his work summarized by Dukore is not matched by the quality of critical analyses of it; as Arnold Hinchliffe suggests, 'A writer must often pray to be saved from his critics and, not least, from those who admire him.'[53] The large body of critical commentary now available on Pinter's work too often confirms some of his fears about language, exhibiting 'stale dead terminology; ideas endlessly repeated and permutated become platitudinous, trite, meaningless'.[54] Mistakes and shortcomings in critical assessments of Pinter's work, however, are sometimes, indirectly, useful in indicating its nature. For example, the response to his drama partly confirms its resemblance to modernism, many of whose texts likewise demanded and frustrated early efforts of interpretation. The excellence of Pinter's plays, and their puzzling quality, similarly encourage attempts at explanation which are nevertheless made problematic by the invalidation of much of the usual apparatus through which analyses are conventionally made, rendered inappropriate by the theatrically innovative mode of Pinter's writing. A resulting characteristic of some

Pinter criticism is a significant abandonment of its analytic, interpretive function in favour of refuge in a vaguer, more metaphoric descriptive language. For example, Almansi and Henderson's recent study conveys some indication of the atmosphere of a Pinter play, but very little about the way this is produced, by its frequent reliance on remarks such as '[Pinter] has only whispered dark words of warning. . . . He has always used words as incantations without letting us know to which religion his rituals belong.'[55]

Such remarks are made particularly disappointing by their appearance in a series of studies of contemporary writers whose editors Malcolm Bradbury and Christopher Bigsby suggest

> We . . . start in the conviction that the age of Beckett . . . Ionesco, Orton, Pinter and Stoppard . . . and many another . . . is a time that has been described as 'post-modern,' in the sense that it is an era consequent to modernism yet different from it.[56]

This is exactly the framework in which Pinter's work is most appropriately considered; that it has so rarely been thoroughly examined in such terms is perhaps a result of a certain insularity among theatre critics and reviewers, reluctant to look beyond the immediate context of the contemporary stage. This has been more or less evident ever since the earliest review of Pinter's drama. Significantly, the most vehement initial rejections of Pinter's plays came from those most initiated in the conventional expectations of the London theatres in which they first appeared. As Harold Hobson recorded in a rare favourable early review of *The Birthday Party*,[57] for example, its reception was much more favourable outside London. Pinter also recalls of this first production of *The Birthday Party* that 'It went on a little tour . . . and was very successful. When it came to London, it was completely massacred by the critics—absolutely slaughtered. I've never really known why.'[58] One possible reason for the 'slack-jawed dismay' of London critics was the particularity of their conditioning in the sort of bourgeois naturalism which dominated earlier decades and whose greatest stronghold remained the West End commercial theatre, where it had only begun to be disturbed in the '50s by the work of Osborne and the

Absurdists. With remarkable uniformity, the reviews which 'absolutely slaughtered' *The Birthday Party* suggested that all its characters were mad[59]; significantly, the only explanation of their unrealistic action available within the framework of a naturalistic view of the play. Still examining the naturalistic surface of the play for 'the message, the moral', and 'what all this means',[60] their familiarity with West-End theatre left early reviewers peculiarly ill-equipped for the challenges to convention presented by Pinter's drama, and for the new strategies therefore required for its appreciation. Some wider awareness of earlier literary developments outside the theatre, and certainly outside the West End theatre, might have prepared them for the apparent oddity of Pinter's work. It is ironic that a particularly damning early review of *The Birthday Party* appeared on the same page of *The Times* as an article entitled 'How Much is Left of Dadaism?'[61]; though Pinter's work may owe little to Dada, the hostile reviewer might have been more tolerant had he borne in mind other equally innovative contemporary developments, especially in the modernist fiction of the 1920s.

Although as Hinchliffe suggests 'The story of Pinter's growth as a dramatist is very much the story of the education of critics and audiences about his particular style', there are signs of a continuing reluctance to assess his work in the broader context of twentieth-century literature. For example, in examining Gregorz Sinko's analysis of *The Birthday Party* in terms of Kafka, Hinchliffe himself suggests

> Such an interpretation seems to me reasonably satisfactory when made by a Polish critic for whom the world of Kafka is not entirely fictional; but it is less so in the context of an English seaside resort. Too strongly the cliché asserts itself: it couldn't happen here . . . . it is the Naturalistic surface of the play that is very strong.[62]

Hinchliffe's remarks, which incidentally ignore the strength of naturalistic surface which is a feature of Kafka's work, exemplify a continuing critical readiness—hardly less limiting in its own way than the insularity of Pinter's earliest reviewers— to pass over Pinter's significant connections with modernist literature, readily believing that 'it couldn't happen here', and ignoring Pinter's own simple suggestion that in certain earlier authors 'something is going on . . . which is going on in me too.' Such surviving critical insularity may best be explained as arising from a readiness among critics to account for the puzzling quality of Pinter's work by mystifying its origins, making the assumption that such strange material in the theatre can have no antecedents elsewhere in literature. Lawrence Kitchin clearly indicated the existence of this sort of error more than twenty years ago in suggesting

> With very few exceptions, the history of English dramatic criticism over the last fifty years has been one of estrangement from modern literature. I can think of no other reason for the difficulty most critics had in placing early Pinter. . . . there are obvious debts to Joyce, via Beckett, to Kafka and to the Hemingway of *The Killers*, perhaps to Eliot's *Sweeney*.[63]

Despite the evident sense of Kitchin's remarks, the difficulty in 'placing' Pinter has not been eradicated, and many critics apparently still prefer to see him as a figure of unique mystery and strangeness. Pinter himself has shown an understandable ennervation with their coinage of the term 'Pinteresque' to refer to his supposedly unique qualities[64]; the assumption that his work is radically innovative, rather than an extension to the stage of earlier literary modes, seriously misrepresents his position, and unnecessarily confuses appreciation of his plays.

Quigley's survey of Pinter criticism rightly points out its failure to provide 'a framework that substantially illuminates his achievement or his individuality', and suggests that a 'further level of generalisation'[65] is required. As Raymond Williams remarks of contemporary drama in general, 'In this confused situation, we need a clear sense of dramatic history and development.'[66] A 'clear sense' of general developments in fiction as well as drama in the twentieth century offers some of the lessons of modernism as alternatives to the 'dead terminology' which has often confused Pinter's reception, and provides a framework, a 'further level of generalisation' from which to examine Pinter's innovation and his indebtedness, his 'achievement or his individuality'. Until Pinter is more widely discussed as 'consequent to modernism' in some of the ways suggested in the earlier part of this essay, the nature of 'one of the best living dramatists', and the real value of his innovations, will continue to be unnecessarily mystified and misunderstood.

NOTES

1. See Austin E. Quigley, *The Pinter Problem* (New Jersey: Princeton University Press, 1975), pp. 5–6, on the failures of Pinter criticism to connect his work with earlier literature.
2. Lawrence M. Bensky, 'Harold Pinter: An Interview', in Arthur Ganz (ed.), *Pinter: A Collection of Critical Essays* (New Jersey: Prentice-Hall, 1972), p. 22.
3. Ernest Hemingway, 'The Killers' (1928), rpt. in *The Essential Hemingway* (St. Albans: Panther, 1977), p. 373.
4. Ibid., p. 368.
5. I.e. Harold Pinter, *Plays*, 4 vols. (London: Eyre Methuen, 1976, 1977, 1978, 1981), Vol. I, p. 152. Subsequent references are to this edition of Pinter's plays.
6. Ernest Hemingway, 'Hills Like White Elephants' (1928), rpt. in *The Essential Hemingway*, p. 364.
7. Ibid., p. 367.
8. Harold Pinter, 'Writing for the Theatre' (Speech to the National Student Drama Festival, 1962) rpt. in *Plays*, Vol. I, pp. 14–15.
9. Ernest Hemingway, *A Farewell to Arms* (1929), rpt. in *The Essential Hemingway*, p. 202.
10. Virginia Woolf, *To the Lighthouse* (1927; rpt. Harmondsworth: Penguin, 1973), p. 202.
11. Quoted in William Baker and Stephen Ely Tabachnik, *Harold Pinter* (Edinburgh: Oliver and Boyd, 1973), p. 13.
12. 'Writing for the Theatre', I. 13.
13. John Russell Brown, *Theatre Language* (London: Allen Lane, 1972), p. 37.
14. Quigley, op. cit., pp. 66, 50.
15. Guido Almansi and Simon Henderson, *Harold Pinter* (London: Methuen, 1983), p. 11.
16. Harold Pinter, 'Writing for Myself', rpt. in *Plays* II. 11.
17. Unsigned review, 'A Simple Play: The Birthday Party on Television', *The Times*, 23 March 1960, p. 16.
18. Franz Kafka, 'The Burrow' (1931), rpt. in *Metamorphosis and Other Stories*, trans. Willa and Edwin Muir (Harmondsworth: Penguin, 1970), pp. 145, 161.
19. Part of Pinter's programme note for the Royal Court Theatre production of *The Room* and *The Dumb Waiter*, 8 March 1960; quoted in Martin Esslin, *Pinter: A Study of his Plays* (London: Methuen, 1973), p. 40.
20. J. L. Styan, *The Dark Comedy* (Cambridge: Cambridge University Press,

1962), pp. 235–36; quoted in Arnold P. Hinchliffe, *Harold Pinter* (Boston: Twayne, 1967), p. 35.

21. Franz Kafka, 'Metamorphosis', in Kafka, op. cit., p. 10. See also G. J. Watson's excellent discussion of this example, and of the connection between Pinter and Kafka generally, in his *Drama: An Introduction* (London: Macmillan, 1983), pp. 189–191.
22. Bensky, op. cit., p. 28.
23. See note 19.
24. Martin Esslin, *The Theatre of the Absurd* (1961; rpt. Harmondsworth: Penguin, 1970), p. 289.
25. Harold Pinter's Introduction to *The Proust Screenplay* (London: Methuen, 1972), p. viii.
26. 'Writing for the Theatre', I. 11.
27. George Wellwarth, *The Theatre of Protest and Paradox* (London: Macgibbon and Kee, 1965) p. 201.
28. Harold Pinter on the B.B.C. Third Programme, quoted in Hinchliffe, op. cit., p. 33.
29. Unsigned article, 'Mr. Harold Pinter: Avant-Garde Playwright and Intimate Review', *The Times*, 16 November 1959, p. 4; and Pinter on the B.B.C. European Service, quoted in Esslin, *Pinter: A Study of his Plays*, p. 36.
30. James R. Hollis, *Harold Pinter: The Poetics of Silence* (Carbondale: Southern Illinois University Press, 1970), p. 42.
31. 'Writing for Myself', II. 9.
32. J. B. Priestley, *Johnson Over Jordan* (London: Heinemann, 1939), p. 133.
33. Ibid., p. 134.
34. Ibid., pp. 129–30.
35. Ibid., pp. 130, 125.
36. Ibid., pp. 120–21.
37. Ronald Hayman, *Harold Pinter* (London: Heinemann, 1968), pp. 23–4.
38. Priestley, op. cit., pp. 22, 25.
39. T. S. Eliot, 'Poetry and Drama', in T. S. Eliot, *On Poetry and Poets* (London: Faber, 1957), p. 87.
40. T. S. Eliot, *The Family Reunion* (1939; rpt. London: Faber, 1976), pp. 97, 111; and T. S. Eliot, *The Cocktail Party* (1950; rpt. London: Faber, 1976), p. 174.
41. Priestley, op. cit., p. 144.
42. Hollis, op. cit., p. 10.
43. Unsigned review, 'Puzzling Surrealism of The Birthday Party', *The Times*, 20 May 1958, p. 3; and Derek Granger, 'The Birthday Party', *Financial Times*, 20 May 1958, p. 15.
44. Bensky, op cit., p. 22; see note 29 for *Times* reference.
45. Ruby Cohn, 'The World of Harold Pinter' in Ganz (ed.), op cit., pp. 78–9.
46. See note 28.
47. Samuel Beckett, *Waiting for Godot* (1956; rpt. London: Faber, 1971), pp. 79, 83.
48. See Hinchliffe, op. cit., p. 171; note 25; and Bensky, op. cit., p. 23.
49. 'Writing for Myself', II. 9.

50. Unsigned review, 'A Slicker and Less Dangerous Pinter', *The Times*, 19 June 1964, p. 18.
51. Priestley, op. cit., p. 124.
52. Bernard Dukore, *Harold Pinter* (London: Methuen, 1982), p. 129.
53. Hinchliffe, op. cit., p. 163.
54. 'Writing for the Theatre', I. 13.
55. Almansi and Henderson, op. cit., p. 13.
56. Ibid., p. 7.
57. 'Life Outside London', *Sunday Times*, 19 June 1958, p. 11.
58. Bensky, op. cit., p. 23.
59. See, for example, reviews in *The Times* (p. 3) and the *Financial Times* (p. 15) of 20 May 1958; and in the *Guardian*, 21 May 1958 (p. 5).
60. *The Times* and the *Financial Times*, as above (note 59).
61. *The Times*, 20 May 1958, p. 3.
62. Hinchliffe, op. cit., pp. 49, 55.
63. Lawrence Kitchin, *Mid-Century Drama* (London: Faber, 1962), p. 119.
64. See Bensky, op. cit., p. 31.
65. Quigley, op. cit., pp. 6, xvii.
66. Raymond Williams, 'Recent English Drama' in Boris Ford (ed.), *The Pelican Guide to English Literature, Volume Seven: The Modern Age* (Harmondsworth: Pelican, 1978), p. 539.

3

Harold Pinter as Screenwriter

by JENNIFER L. RANDISI

Harold Pinter has been equated with the theatre of the absurd, the theatre of cruelty, the theatre of situation and the comedy of menace. His work has been called naturalistic, realistic, existential, supra-realistic, impressionistic and compression-istic.[1] Although most critics have not agreed how to define Pinter's work, they have agreed that in it form is content. When Beckett said of *Finnegans Wake* that Joyce's 'writing is not *about* something; *it is that something*'[2] he was remarking the extent to which it is possible for the two to intersect. Where the earlier Joyce novel *Ulysses* relies on mythic patterning, *Finnegans Wake* relies on verbal patterning. And this is a crucial difference. In repeating the journey of Odysseus, Leopold Bloom maintains a connection to the past (even if the repetition is a parody of the original action). In *Finnegans Wake*, the repetition is verbal. The novel's only connection is to its own language and that language is constantly changing.

Pinter's attitude toward language is paradoxical. He both respects and distrusts it.

> I have mixed feelings about words myself. Moving among them, sorting them out, watching them appear on the page, from this I derive a considerable pleasure. But at the same time I have another strong feeling about words which amounts to nothing less than nausea. Such a weight of words confronts us day in, day out, words spoken in a context such as this, words written by me

and by others, the bulk of it a stale dead terminology; ideas endlessly repeated and permutated become platitudinous, trite, meaningless.[3]

Words are what we use to communicate, but their ability to communicate is suspect. As Faulkner's Addie Bundren says in *As I Lay Dying*, a word is 'just a shape to fill a lack'.[4] Pinter is interested in both shape and lack. In his adaptations and original screenplays, the shape is the cinematic pattern of language and silence while the lack is the inability of characters to be consistent.

Clive Donner said of the completed film of *The Caretaker* that 'all comes from the text.'

> Of course, the silences are really the things that *make* that particular work of Pinter's. I remember Harold said to me one day, 'You know, it's the shape of the pauses that's important.' And once you've got that, then you have a series of fascinating images with three highly contrasting characters: all of them give you a particular line on how you should photograph them, and where they should be in relation to one another, whether they're facing one another or not.[5]

Further, each scene within every screenplay has a shape. A scene from early in *The Quiller Memorandum* is representative.

> But listen . . . what kind of people are they exactly? Nazis?
>
> INGE. Well, they are . . . I would say. But of course they don't call themselves that any more.
>
> QUILLER. They don't?
>
> INGE. No
>
> QUILLER. You know, this fits in with what this man was telling me. He was saying that these boys don't show themselves, they keep themselves pretty much under cover.
>
> INGE. Yes. So I believe.
>
> QUILLER. Yes . . . he was saying they've got a kind of long term policy, that they want to infiltrate themselves into the mind of the country, over a period of years. But they're not in any kind of hurry, this time . . . you know . . .
>
> *He laughs.*
>
> INGE. Yes.
>
> QUILLER. But that they're very convinced men. Very convinced.

INGE. I would say that, yes.
QUILLER. Yes, that's exactly what this man was telling me.

Pause.

INGE. Who is this man?

He looks up from his drink.

QUILLER. What man?
INGE. The man . . . who was talking to you.
QUILLER. Oh, just a guy I met in a bar.
INGE. Oh.

Pause.

Are you going to write about this . . . question . . . in your article?
QUILLER. No, no, it's outside my range. I'm not political. I haven't got a political brain.
INGE. Ah.

They drink.[6]

The alternation of language and pause defines the nature of the communication between Quiller and Inge about Nazi activity in Germany. The conversation begins with the cut to Inge's flat and ends with a long pause indicated by the direction 'they drink', even though the scene and dialogue continue. According to Pinter,

> The pause is a pause because of what has just happened in the minds and guts of the characters. They spring out of the text. They're not formal conveniences or stresses but part of the body of the action.[7]

The final shape *The Quiller Memorandum* takes is a combination of the shapes of its individual scenes. Although she does not like the film, Pauline Kael senses this literacy.

> . . . *Quiller* was actually scripted by Harold Pinter. It doesn't have a shred of plausibility, its clichés are not freshened by any original touches, it hasn't a memorable character or a witty line, and yet in some preposterous way it *is* literate.[8]

63

In Pinter's screenplays literacy is largely a matter of form.

Aston and Davies (*The Caretaker*), Leo and Mrs. Maudsley (*The Go-Between*), Jo and Jake (*The Pumpkin Eater*), Emma and Jerry (*Betrayal*)—virtually all of Pinter's characters reveal themselves in the patterns of their words and silences. Pauses and silences are so important, in fact, that Pinter's screenplays often end on them: *The Caretaker* closes with Davies' fragmented speech and final silence; *The Go-Between* ends on Marian's incomplete thought, 'Tell him—'. Pinter has said that 'when true silence falls we are still left with echo but are nearer nakedness. One way of looking at speech is to say that it is a constant strategy to cover nakedness.'⁹ Characters rely on patterns of language and silence because, as Addie Bundren says, they 'fill a lack'. The lack Pinter's screen characters try to fill is their inability to remain fixed. Like the rest of us, Pinter's characters contradict themselves, reveal only what they choose to reveal, and confuse each other with language. In *The Pumpkin Eater*, for example, Jake's responses are stratagems rather than answers.

> Jo. Did you sleep with Philpot?
> JAKE. Oh, Christ, it's years ago, it's gone—
> Jo. Did you?
> JAKE. Yes, of course I did.
> Jo. You told me you hadn't.
> JAKE. I lied. So what? What else did you expect me to do?
> Jo. Here? In the house?
> JAKE. I don't remember. Yes.
> Jo. Often?
> JAKE. As often as we could. What's the point? What the hell does it matter?
> Jo. What about all the others?
> JAKE. What others?
> Jo. The others.
> JAKE. There weren't any others.
> Jo. How many?
> JAKE. Half a dozen. A dozen. I don't know. What does the number matter?
> Jo. When you were away, or when you were here?
> JAKE. When I was away! Is that what you want me to say?
> Jo. If it's true.
> JAKE. Then it was while I was away.¹⁰

Neither character can verify his or her version of what happened between Jake and Philpot, and we do not know any more 'truth' at the end of the exchange than we did at the beginning. Connection is not to action in the past, but rather to language in the present.

It is the collaboration between shape and lack that creates a situation (what *is*), whether or not the situation happens to be true. Inconsistency is a character's failure (or refusal) to verify another's point of view.

> The desire for verification on the part of all of us, with regard to our own experience and the experience of others, is understandable but cannot always be satisfied. I suggest there can be no hard distinctions between what is real and what is unreal, nor between what is true and what is false; it can be both true and false.[11]

The most we can hope for, therefore, is to perceive what is revealed in any given moment. We can, for example, understand what Aston tells us about himself in *The Caretaker* but, as Pinter tells us, 'it isn't necessary to conclude that everything Aston says about his experiences in the mental hospital is true.'[12] If character is not fixed, then reality ceases to exist.

> A moment is sucked away and distorted, often at the time of its birth. We will all interpret a common experience quite differently, though we prefer to subscribe to the view that there's a shared common ground, a known ground. I think there's a shared common ground, all right, but that it's more like a quicksand. Because 'reality' is quite a strong firm word we tend to think, or to hope, that the state to which it refers is equally firm, settled and unequivocal. It doesn't seem to be, and in my opinion, it's no worse or better for that.[13]

In *The French Lieutenant's Woman*, for example, the situation (what *is*) is the very equivocal sum of shape and lack times two.

> ANNA *in her caravan. A knock on the door.*

> ANNA. Hello!

> MIKE *comes in.*

> MIKE. May I introduce myself?

65

ANNA. I know who you are.

They smile. He closes the door.

So you prefer to walk alone?
    ANNA. Me? Not me. Her.
    MIKE. I enjoyed that.
    ANNA. What?
    MIKE. Our exchange. Out there.
    ANNA. Did you? I never know . . .
    MIKE. Know what?
    ANNA. Whether it's any good.
    MIKE. Listen. Do you find me—?
    ANNA. What?
    MIKE. Sympathetic.
    ANNA. Mmn. Definitely.
    MIKE. I don't mean me. I mean him.
    ANNA. Definitely.
    MIKE. But you still prefer to walk alone?
    ANNA. Who? Me—or her?
    MIKE. Her. You like company.

He strokes the back of her neck.

Don't you?
    ANNA. (*Smiling*). Not always. Sometimes I prefer to walk
alone.[14]

Here, the confusion and uncertainty surrounding Sarah and
Charles is compounded by the confusion and uncertainty
surrounding Anna and Mike. Charles (Mike's character)
refers to Sarah (Anna's character) as 'my sweet . . . mystery';
Anna tells Mike 'it's all so unreal.'[15] There are two realities
here (the film and the film within the film) neither of which is
necessarily true.

Identity thus becomes a function of the mind or, more
precisely, a function of the point of view of the perceiver in
relation to the object perceived. We only exist in relation to
others. As Walter Kerr observes, 'Pinter believes that this is
the way life *is*, that it's only by contending with the other
person in the void that we arrive at some kind of identity.'[16]
Pinter expresses this in his opening remarks to an audience:

So I'm speaking with some reluctance, knowing that there are at least twenty-four possible aspects of any single statement, depending on where you're standing at the time or on what the weather's like. A categorical statement, I find, will never stay where it is and be finite. It will immediately be subject to modification by the other twenty-three possibilities of it.[17]

And this is where form and content intersect. Very little happens in a Pinter screenplay; what *does* happen is collaboration.

Pinter has said 'what goes on in my plays is realistic, but what I'm doing is not realism.'[18] Pinter's films accentuate this distinction by providing real backdrops against which we view characters moving realistically. Yet the result is not realism. As Pinter has said of *Accident*, 'in this film, everything happens, nothing is explained. It has been pared down and down.'[19] Screenwriter, cinematographer, director, actor collaborate to create realistic fiction—fiction more true than fact because heightened and intensified. Pinter likes Joseph Losey's direction for precisely this reason.

No elaborations, no odd angles, no darting about. Just a level intense look at people, at things. As though if you look at them hard enough they will give up their secrets.[20]

The problem, of course, is that people don't 'give up their secrets' as we view them. Rather, the more characters talk the less we feel we know them. What we experience is a verbal hologram, a structure dependent upon the collaboration of different points of view.

Pinter's verbal holograms usually involve two or three people. Two characters tend either to reverse rôles or to fight to preserve them; three is the number necessary for betrayal. *The Basement* and *The Servant* are the best examples of rôle reversal. By the end of *The Basement*, Scott and Law have traded places: Law is the intruder in possession of Jane, Scott occupies the room. Similarly, by the end of *The Servant*, Barrett has become master and Tony his servant. Of this kind of reversal Pinter has said,

A threat is constantly there; it's got to do with this question of being in the uppermost position, or attempting to be. That's something of what attracted me to do the screenplay of *The*

67

Servant, which was someone else's story, you know. I wouldn't call this violence so much as a battle for positions, it's a very common, everyday thing.[21]

The alternative to switching position is fighting to preserve it. Barrett knows more about Tony's weaknesses than Tony knows about his and, often in Pinter's screenplays, the more a character knows the more dominant that character is. Asked why the conversations in his plays are so effective, Pinter replied: 'I think possibly it's because people fall back on anything they can lay their hands on verbally to keep away from the danger of knowing, and of being known.'[22] If knowledge brings danger it also brings power, and that is why Pinter's characters often try to keep from being known. Marian's response to her guests in *The Go-Between* is just such a stratagem. By answering statement with question, Marian remains unfixed, unidentified.

> *They all move to the door.*

> A GUEST. You were in cracking form to-day at croquet, Marian.
> MARIAN. Was I?
> DENYS. Marian is quite formidable at croquet.
> MARIAN. Am I?[23]

This exchange may strike us as funny, but, as Pinter explains, 'more often than not the speech only *seems* to be funny—the man in question is actually fighting a battle for his life.'[24] Robert and Jerry in *Betrayal*, Stephen and Charley in *Accident*, Quiller and Oktober in *The Quiller Memorandum*, Jake and Jo in *The Pumpkin Eater*—all use language to protect themselves from others.

Conversations that involve three people almost always lead to betrayal. When Mick enters *The Caretaker*, when McCann and Goldberg enter *The Birthday Party*, when Robert enters *Betrayal*, the collaboration becomes three-sided and, in Pinter's work, three is a very dangerous number. Betrayal is often something we hear rather than see. In *The Caretaker*, for example, Davies' betrayal of both Mick and Aston is one of intention rather than action, and it is revealed by what he says not by what he does. Similarly, Stanley in *The Birthday Party* is only guilty to the extent that we believe the accusations of Goldberg and McCann, and the same is true of Jake and Philpot in *The Pumpkin Eater*.

What happens (the verbal hologram) is therefore dependent upon the form the collaboration takes. Collaboration can take three forms: saying makes it so (meaningful repetition), saying does not make it so (meaningless repetition), and saying as aggression. Petey and Meg's conversation about cornflakes in *The Birthday Party* is an example of meaningful repetition. Meg derives a great sense of well-being from Petey's repeated assurances that the cornflakes are 'very nice' because saying makes it so; saying defines a reality. The conversation between Jerry and Emma which opens *Betrayal* is a similar definition, a mutual reassurance that both are, in fact, 'all right'. Conway's eulogy of the 'honest tradesman' in *The Pumpkin Eater* works in a slightly different way. Saying, for Conway, is an assertion of value, the location of a moral centre in an immoral landscape.

As often as not, however, saying does not make it so. Law's repeated question 'Wouldn't you say the flat is a little small, for three people?' is rendered meaningless by Scott's 'No. No. Not at all.' Because Scott refuses to agree (to let saying make it so), he assumes control of the flat. Like Law, Stanley of *The Birthday Party* loses control he possessed earlier in the film. His wishful 'They won't come' is contradicted by the arrival of Goldberg and McCann. And in *The Pumpkin Eater*, Jo's inability to come to terms with Ingram's vacation is reflected in her refusal to accept what he tells her.

> . . . I won't be seeing you for a couple of weeks. Just chew it over, and take the pills of course.
> Jo. Couple of weeks?
> INGRAM. Oh, I'm sorry, haven't I told you? We're off to Gstaadt on Friday for a spot of skiing. It's my great passion, I'm afraid.
> Jo. Skiing?
> INGRAM. Oh, and cut down on liquids as much as you can. Can we make an appointment for the . . . 19th?
> Jo. Can't make it. No . . . can't make the 19th.[25]

Jo's questions are not questions at all, but rather statements indicating loss of control. As such, they are reminiscent of

Davies's hopeless lament in *The Caretaker*, 'if only the weather would break'.

Saying is also a form of aggression. Stanley is verbally tortured by Goldberg and McCann in *The Birthday Party*, just as Davies is the victim of Mick's language in *The Caretaker*.

> DAVIES. Me? Now wait a minute—wait a minute—you got the wrong man.
> MICK. How could I have the wrong man? You're the only man I've spoken to. You're the only man I've told, about my dreams, about my deepest wishes, you're the only one I've told, and I only told you because I understood you were an experienced first-class professional interior and exterior decorator.
> DAVIES. Now look here—
> MICK. You mean you wouldn't know how to fit teal-blue, copper and parchment linoleum squares and have those colours re-echoed in the walls?[26]

Jo, of *The Pumpkin Eater*, is subjected to a verbal attack by a woman at the hairdresser's, and dialogue turns to aggression when Quiller encounters three potential antagonists in *The Quiller Memorandum*.

The cinematic counterpart to the verbal hologram is the montage. Most of the shifts in time and place found in Pinter's adaptations are visual equivalents of the original first person narrator. *Accident, The Servant, The Go-Between, The Proust Screenplay, The Last Tycoon* and *The French Lieutenant's Woman* all required a replacement for the original first person narrative voice. In scripting *Accident*, Pinter recalls

> I couldn't find a direct film equivalent to the free-association, stream-of-consciousness style of the novel. It's precious, self-conscious, over-elaborate on film. You should be able to convey the same sort of apprehension not by opening out . . . but by closing in, looking closer and closer, harder and harder at things that are before you.[27]

The greatest narrative challenges, however, were *The French Lieutenant's Woman* and *The Proust Screenplay*. Compressing John Fowles's 366-page novel into a two hour screenplay was seriously complicated by the narrator's presentation of two possible endings. The solution Pinter and director Karel Riesz hit upon was the device of the film within the film: the film maintains the second ending; the film within the film, the first. The difficulty of preserving the narrative voice remained, however, and was only solved by, in Fowles's words, Pinter's 'truly remarkable gift for reducing the long and complex without distortion'.[28]

The task was even greater in condensing Proust's *À la Recherche du Temps Perdu* into a 177-page screenplay. Pinter writes in his introduction,

> If the thing was to be done at all, one would have to try to distill the whole book into an integrated whole. With this Joe [Losey] and Barbara [Bray] agreed. We decided that the architecture of the film should be based on two main and contrasting principles: one, a movement chiefly narrative, toward disillusion, and the other, more intermittent, toward revelation, rising to where time that was lost is found, and fixed forever in art.[29]

The technique Pinter uses is the montage, and the effect, by the end of the screenplay, is that one plus one equals three; the montage (a collaboration of time and space which defines what *is*) is larger than the sum of its parts. The splicing of past and present in *The Go-Between*, *The Pumpkin Eater*, *The French Lieutenant's Woman* and *The Proust Screenplay* both intensifies and enlarges the original action: voice over and cuts to Colton in *The Go-Between* bring the past into alignment with the present by the end of the film; only by cutting from Jo's movements in the present to her actions in the past does the present derive meaning in *The Pumpkin Eater*; *The French Lieutenant's Woman*'s Sarah and Charles achieve a fuller definition in the nineteenth century through Anna and Mike in the twentieth; the movement toward revelation in *The Proust Screenplay* is only significant when set against the narrative movement toward disillusion. As Pinter remarks in his introduction,

> When Marcel, in *Le Temps Retrouvé*, says that he is now able to start his work, he has already written it. We have just read it. Somehow this remarkable conception had to be found again in another form.[30]

When the audience encounters a repeated image or a parallel scene, the effect is to alter, to amplify, the original. Meaning (the 'three' of my earlier formula) is therefore a product of collaboration (the 'one plus one').

Meaning (content) and collaboration (form) join in Pinter's notion of balance. It is important that *Accident* begin and end with the same sound track, just as it is important that both the first and second ending of *The French Lieutenant's Woman* finish with the same word, 'Sarah!' Pinter has said that 'for me, everything has to do with shape, structure, and over-all unity.'[31] Over-all unity is crucial because, as Beckett said of Joyce's novel, a Pinter screenplay 'is not *about* something; *it is that something.*' According to Pinter,

> ... the key word is economy, economy of movement and gesture, of emotion and its expression, both the internal and the external in specific and exact relation to each other, so that there is no wastage and no mess.[32]

Everything in a Pinter screenplay counts, but only in relation to everything else. The changes in the decoration of the room in *The Basement* are only significant in relation to one another; the red ball and beer stain in *The Pumpkin Eater* only gain meaning in what has happened between the first and second time we see them; Torcello and modern literature become ways of talking about love and adultery in *Betrayal*. The placement of paintings in a room, a child's red ball, a trip to Torcello are made epiphanic by the way they recur in the film. In a Pinter screenplay, meaning is cumulative. And, like Proust's Marcel, we only begin to see when our vision is complete.

NOTES

1. Herman T. Schroll, *Harold Pinter: A Study of His Reputation (1958–1969) and a Checklist* (Metuchen, New Jersey: Scarecrow Press, Inc., 1971), p. 7.
2. Bernard F. Dukore, *Harold Pinter* (New York: Grove Press, Inc., 1982), p. 7.
3. Harold Pinter, 'Writing for the theatre', in *Complete Works: One* (New York: Grove Press, Inc., 1977), p. 13.
4. William Faulkner, *As I Lay Dying* (New York: Modern Library, 1967), p. 164.
5. *Voices of Film Experience, 1894 to the present*, ed. Jay Leyda (New York: Macmillan Publishing Co., Inc., 1977), pp. 111 and 112 respectively.

6. Harold Pinter, *The Quiller Memorandum*, in *Five Screenplays* (New York: Grove Press, 1978), pp. 158–59.

7. Steven H. Gale, *Butter's Going Up: A Critical Analysis of Harold Pinter's Work* (Durham, North Carolina: Duke University Press, 1977), p. 273.

8. Pauline Kael, *Kiss Kiss Bang Bang* (Boston: Little, Brown and Co., 1968), p. 11.

9. Harold Pinter, 'Writing for the theatre', p. 14.

10. Harold Pinter, *The Pumpkin Eater*, in *Five Screenplays*, pp. 120–21.

11. Harold Pinter, 'Writing for the theatre', p. 11.

12. 'Harold Pinter', in *Writers at Work: The Paris Review Interviews*, 3rd Series (New York: Viking Press, 1967), p. 362.

13. Harold Pinter, 'Writing for the theatre', p. 11.

14. Harold Pinter, *The French Lieutenant's Woman, A Screenplay* (Boston: Little, Brown and Company, 1981), pp. 25–6.

15. Harold Pinter, *The French Lieutenant's Woman, A Screenplay*, pp. 72 and 67.

16. *Playwrights, Lyricists, Composers, on the Theater*, ed. Otis L. Guernsey, Jr. (New York: Dodd, Mead and Co., 1974), p. 384.

17. Harold Pinter, 'Writing for the theatre', p. 9.

18. Harold Pinter, 'Writing for Myself', in *Complete Works: Two* (New York: Grove Press, 1977), p. 11.

19. Foster Hirsch, *Joseph Losey* (Boston: Twayne Publishers, 1980), p. 119.

20. Foster Hirsch, *Joseph Losey*, p. 121.

21. 'Harold Pinter', in *Writers at Work: The Paris Review Interviews*, p. 363.

22. *Writers at Work*, p. 360.

23. Harold Pinter, *The Go-Between*, in *Five Screenplays*, p. 291.

24. Austin E. Quigley, *The Pinter Problem* (Princeton, New Jersey: Princeton University Press, 1975), p. 52.

25. Harold Pinter, *The Pumpkin Eater*, in *Five Screenplays*, pp. 90–1.

26. Harold Pinter, *The Caretaker*, in *Complete Works: Two*, p. 81.

27. Foster Hirsch, *Joseph Losey*, p. 119.

28. Harold Pinter, *The French Leiutenant's Woman, A Screenplay*, p. xi.

29. Harold Pinter, *The Proust Screenplay* (New York: Grove Press, Inc., 1977), p. ix.

30. Harold Pinter, *The Proust Screenplay*, p. x.

31. *Writers at Work*, p. 367.

32. Harold Pinter, 'Introduction', in *Complete Works: Four* (New York: Grove Press, Inc., 1981), p. xii.

4

Pinter's Stagecraft: Meeting People is Wrong

by STANLEY EVELING

The term 'experimental', as applied to mid-twentieth century drama, does not adequately describe the attempt to get away from certain structural dramatic metaphors embedded and unexamined until then. These temporary bits and pieces of dramatic meaning became questionable props in the light of the things it seemed necessary to say and do with drama and were sensitive to social change. Some dramatists dispensed with the standardized presentation of work within a fixed set, within the statuesque framework of the proscenium arch, and instead utilized Open Spaces, rounded acting areas and Traverse theatres. This allowed for a much greater flexibility, a nimbleness of presentation, a quicker, subtler flow of dramatic happenings, a cinematic fluidity but also indicated a way of life that was supposed to be in a constant and turbulent flux. Some dramatists also dropped the secure relationship and associated responsibilities of the author, director and the actors in favour of a more interrelated, less rôle-constituted arrangement. Yet another casualty of change was the concept of the audience logically and hence psychologically insulated from the imaginary goings on.

To all these radical happenings Pinter's plays remained indifferent, not hostile; simply passing them by. A Pinter play is happy to be put on stage in a standard stage environment, even emphatic in its wish to present the action as taking place in a conventionally understood domestic scene. Audience, actors, directors and writers stay put and proscenium arches stay firmly in place. But, of course, it is the aggressive contrast between the normal and the abnormal uses to which the characters are put which constitutes the work's basic metaphor.

Nor has Pinter been at all ostensibly concerned with political matters, with plays as political agents advocating remedial alterations and deconstructions of the standard scene. Pinter's people do not look outward but inward, at each other, and askance. He does not, then, at least in the surfaces of his plays, speak as a radical this or that. Whatever takes place inside his audiences, there is no direct signal from the plays that political meaning is around. Pinter's plays are not, on the face of it, either political or moral acts, except in the tediously trite sense in which everything can be claimed to be so.

But in other, more complicated ways they do belong to, are at the centre of innovation, subversive transformations and alterations in how plays signify—though I shall try to suggest, not prove (since in these matters how does a proof go), that his plays exist in order that nothing shall happen, that no real change shall take place. So beyond the changes to which he has remained totally impervious there are these other innovative manoeuvres to interpret which put his work into that class of odd modern objects to which the work of Beckett, Genet, Ionesco, Adamov, Orton, Heathcoate Williams and others belongs. Two things distinguish this contribution to the twentieth-century repertoire. One is the way in which the plot is used or, rather, how the image or decayed presence of the plot operates; and the other has to do with the irresistible rise of sub-plot people to positions of dramatic power and dominance, a radical change in the character and social status of the heroic personnel.

The two are connected, since sub-plot people are essentially marginal existents, hangers-on at the primary feast who move around the main action with crumbs to pick at and are not deeply implicated in anything. Sub-plots make no large or highly regarded points; sub-plot denizens are not the ultimate repositories of a play's values. So it is odd to find them, in mid-twentieth century drama, trying to have a life of their own, at the play's centre, more or less unaltered, uncomfortably thrust into the limelight, having to make do with the same sort of lightweight eventfulness that is their allotted dramatic portion in life and without the solemn strength of main-plot existence to lean on.

To establish what is odd and innovative here, what this bizarre state of affairs amounts to—to make, at least, a decent guess at what's afoot and amiss—it is helpful to look at what is lost when mainplot persons go missing, when traditional dramatic options (and what is the same thing classfied, high comedy, farce and tragedy) are rejected. A marxist or radical interpretation has its temptations here. At least part of the story for some playwrights may be that their work is a reflection and a facilitating device in the complex social alterations of recent years, reflecting both those who have and those who have sought power or the right to be heard. Sub-plot people are, after all, images of servitude, belong to a stratum deprived of rights and privileges, exist only in virtue of their limited ability to help to keep main-plot narration going. As social power has spread or a demand for it has surfaced, become the possession of or is claimed by more and more from the 'lower depths', so drama throughout the West has introduced into its cast-lists these claimants to and new owners of authority. Events move from the courts to the drawing-rooms, from there to the market-place, even the hovel, prisons, mounds of mud. Those whom drama takes seriously alter to accommodate social alteration, the novel speaks of and to women and in Dickens the working class begins its powerful intrusion, albeit still with a strong, sub-plot atmosphere around it, still prone to anxiety-ridden, Dickensian distortion typical of its sub-plot past.

In the present century, with the pace of change and upward mobility increasing, for whatever reason, there have been severe changes in cast-list persons; tramps, lunatics, sexual deviants, figures of oddity and menace have trooped into the theatre and onto its stage. So here, and not surprisingly, the favoured twentieth-century plot, associated with this sub-versive genre, a parable of accepted or rejected change, has been of the intruder or disruptive and inscrutable stranger arriving into a set piece, traditionally organized situation and threatening to overturn it. This intruder plot, handled with comic menace and a lot of reassuring comic tact, processes both an anxiety and a willingness or, sometimes, a mollifying refusal to accept these novel incomers. Drama has existed here to handle, in an acceptable fictional atmosphere, since what is not happening before one's very eyes is a manageable threat, the problem of what to do. Through laughter, the dangerous becomes welcomed or excluded without—as it were—giving offence. In the latter case, a rarity in an era when the great majority have taken up positions on the left, where the creative impulse is conservative, as, I shall argue, is the case with Pinter, the intruder enters only to be ejected again, I think here of *The Caretaker*.

But disarming and persuasive as such an account can be made to seem, the depicting of sub-plot intruders into main-plot arenas as a reflection of and participation in the battles for social freedom or the keeping of social power, I do not think that such an intention is more than contributory in Pinter's case. His conservativism is an effect of other concealed causes and not the main item on the agenda. To see what else is going on, not merely, I think, in Pinter but in others too, I propose to take a quick glance in the direction of lost options, the great paradigms of traditional dramatic effort and to attempt something in the line of explanation as to what was lost and gained or gained and lost by not taking these standard routes to dramatic meaning, by bringing perplexed sub-plot peripherals to the centre of the modern stage.

I begin with high comedy. Here we have to mention a troublesome ambiguity in the concept of comedy itself, a tendency to associate comedy with the comical. But high comedy is not for the sake of laughter. Perhaps nothing is—laughter is still an unexplained phenomenon—but high comedy does not need it to make its point, does not exploit the merely comical, the laughable, the bizarre, the peculiar, the crestfallen, the accidental, as its special means. On the contrary, it is at home with high pretensions and clear-sighted aims. It may use part of the disreputable and the odd as part of its surface, as inducements and entreaties to appropriate responses, but these are not central to its aim, its line of fire. High comedy is a serious matter and its central figures are shielded from our laughter. Even *The Taming of the Shrew*, though the plot device is a means to the ritual humiliation of its splendid woman, has high human norms as its end, though norms we now find it hard to accept, even within the protected confines of a work of art. Plays of the high comic kind are about the solemn business of ends being pursued and achieved and this by morally and socially acceptable means and essentially by these means. High comedy is about the conditions of human thriving, human nature in its tight-rope walk across the abyss to felicity and rewards. Its postulate is Socratically optimistic and its plots are the persuasive devices by means of which it is proved that good efforts lead to good consequences, efforts which produce what they aim at, are willed attempts towards an agreed end. The aim is to confirm and verify the Socratic optimism which holds that knowledge, virtue and well-being walk side by side, hand in glove.

Dramatists and novelists struggle with this recalcitrant hypothesis in many different ways. Not many can manage Jane Austen's firm and elegant certainty that, give or take a hiccup or two, the well-intentioned and the spiritually well-endowed will do well and that those who are neither will not. Both Shakespeare and Molière tempt this providence, wrestle with a Cartesian doubt as to the validity of the high comic mode and are, therefore, more to a threatened taste. Both flirt with the idea of comic success under extreme threat, both just about block unhappy outcomes by means which require all the majestic duplicity and sheer comic style at their unique command. What saves *Measure for Measure*, if it is saved, is, in part, the full flowing verse. I am not so sure that *All's Well that Ends Well*, self-conciously announcing the perilously moral notion that what comes out well is well done succeeds. Molière is arrogantly cynical to the point where his satirical power threatens comic hope, as in *Tartuffe*, and, in *Don Juan*, a tragic hero struggles to come out from under the comic wraps. No serious twentieth-century talent works within the high comic shape: the last, maybe uneasily, was Tolstoy whose *Anna Karenina* is a victim offered up to a relentlessly high comic idea, that her demise is not tragic but morally deserved. Here is an immense work sensitive to great strains, those which are, finally, to make these traditional options untenable. The next serious move, so to say, is made by Chekhov. His *Ivanov* is the representation of a tragic hero with a comic soul, whose death, therefore, is not tragic but not merely comic either. With this character, a twentieth-century ambiguity arrives. Where competence, will, knowledge of good and evil, social and moral ways and means, the rational plot or its magic simulacrum, as in later Shakespeare and Molière, are not the issue but where plot marches its characters to a happy concluding moment, we move towards farce.

Farce is the last desperate solution to the problem of comedy, of life, short, that is, of the tragic. In farce the artist takes on the whole responsibility, since farce is the most purely artistic solution to the problem of the happy end. There the whole problem is taken up by the artist, his ingenuity constructing an account of things which manufactures or suspends belief. Farce under-rates without despising human intentions and human nature, since, of necessity, dignity is lost when what happens is not a consequence of humanly directed power. Dignity is lost but the human bacon is saved. In farce its purposes are achieved through laughter. We must never be threatened by seriousness for, in this invented environment, reason must not come in and only by being an idiot does one succeed. Construed rather mechanically characters here are mirror-like inversions of the high comic, blessed by ignorance and armoured in incompetence. Under these strict conditions, circumstances relent. Here human nature is delivered into the artist's hands, is insulated by art's music from real disaster. Nothing really threatens since no recognizably large issues are allowed to arise or, better, no issue that arises is allowed to seem large. Farcical figures do not perceive large things and they themselves are beneath or beyond admiration. Contrivance here achieves nothing, though it does, of course, produce effects. In pure farce, accident becomes purposive and this has to be so if the buffoons of life are to get by. As the comic inverse of high comedy, success attends the incompetent, and not to know is to be in a state of grace. There is, here, an ultimate bottom line assurance that, even though human skills mock their possessors, objects, things, brute facts, events themselves, the objective plot will connive in the innocent's favour. Rhyme and reason are not human, a blind divinity doth shape these ends, rough-hew them how we will.

Farces make fools of lofty consciousness but rescue the poor mammal below.

The mangled quote suggests, also, that if farce upends high comedy, it has ideological connections with the tragic, for farce also images the tragic plot. In both what takes place is beyond far-sighted control; events take their own course and cannot be altered. But, whereas in tragedy fate draws all things to an irremediable and catastrophic close, in farce the topsy-turvy logic of unreasonable optimism prevails. In tragedy the fates kill; in farce they change into the friendly ones.

In farce, then, as in tragedy, its characters are very busy and quick in not controlling events. Farcical and tragic figures solve mere riddles to be confronted with mysteries. Farce undermines human dignity and its favoured people are fools. In tragedy, too, its immense central figures run this same criticizing risk, since the tragic plot always exhibits a failure on the part of the tragic character to cope, to bend the world's will. The tragic artist, therefore, always dallies with the rational idea that the outcomes are merited by some designatable tragic flaw, by some feature of the human spirit, even at its best, a rashness, being a fond and foolish old man, a strumpet's fool, being mad, like Hamlet, maybe, or Pentheus, being absolute and fixed, beyond commonsense, like Antigone. Oedipus is blind when he sees, sees clearly when he is blinded. Othello is a magnificent dupe. Yet it would be fatal to the tragic enterprise if such figures were to be seen as less than paradigms of human value. Farce diminishes but tragedy elevates. In farces fools thrive. In tragedy the great fail, transcend foolishness and bring things to where they always are. Tragedy, in line with Schopenhauer's perception of it, persuades us to give up slight hopes; this is how the plot works, being the progress of the reluctant hero to an ordained end. In the last real tragedy we have, Ibsen's *Hedda Gabler*, the plot is the chronicle of a reluctance to take on the tragic rôle. Those to whom it is offered decline it, and hence decline into comic, contriving, self-trivializing figures. Then she fully recognizes who she is, which character tragedy has in mind. This is the tragic becoming self-conscious before it vanishes as a form of art; the presentation, in the ostensible plot (Hamlet's delaying is another version of this mandatory reluctance), of a will to such a death that human value is re-established.

One last point. In the tragic mode the tragic idea is best realized in a domestic setting. Superficially it is odd, perhaps, that plays that have to do with large-scale lives and happenings, matters of life and death, rarely happen where epic, heroic events are at hand. Battle may be joined, but it is the murder of friends, death of wives, with those who resemble our fathers as they slept, that constitute the tragic occasion. Normal disaster is not to the point. Tragic heroes and heroines die in, are undermined by, domestic circumstance; things tragically happen in the vicinity of wives, fathers, brothers, uncles, where there are ties of blood. To gather together these tell-tale signs and to see to what they all point would be to have a theory of the tragic. This is another, larger matter, perhaps. I leave it there.

What these three traditional modes have in common is a sense of order, whether of an imposed human, moral or God-endowed order or of a fateful or whimsical order in things. Order is what constitutes the organizing brain of such drama, explicates the form of existence of those to whom it applies. The ways in which the characters live is an effect of how they relate to this objective frame, the organizing web. Around this central frame, however—at least in the case of the high comic and the tragic, the main plot and its primary persons, the repositories of a play's beliefs—there is, often, a kind of unserious, lightweight hubbub of minor beings and a sub-plot circumstance and its own inter-relations which only tangentially collide with and impinge upon the higher goings-on. Its figures do have some main-plot relevance but usually as go-betweens, causers of minor happenings, twists and turns in mainstream matters. Their destinies are not the main event of the dramatic evening; what befalls them is a minor matter at the edges of relevance. Or so it seems. They seem, on the whole, to operate as light-weight relief from central seriousness but, maybe, they perform a more serious rôle. It is more likely that they are the necessary remnants of the Greek chorus, whatever function that is there to perform. Certainly they belong to a lower order of being. They lack weight. More importantly, for present Pinter-like purposes, the temper and the values of their mirror-like existence are the risible shadows of rôles and values ratified and demonstrated at the play's centre. They lack power, have no real responsibility except as adjuncts to main-plot purposes. They possess vicarious value and, lacking power or high status in the pecking order, they must operate by means of lower tactics, substitute for real authority bombast, for wisdom cunning and duplicity, the resources of underdogs. Nevertheless, despite all these negations, they possess humour, vivacity and energy and can, therefore, come to exert pressures on main plot life, make its high seriousness appear questionable, posit alien criteria, a certain anarchic, amoral or immoral point of view. Beyond responsibility, beyond being able to rise above a predetermined social point, they become images of a certain sort of simplicity, sometimes earthy and natural, sometimes threatening or absurd. Order lies beyond them and where power is. So like Caliban's, their mimetic lives come across as yearnings for the higher and, like Caliban, can seem like a threat to main-plot cruelty and pretension. Their presence, beneath this pretension, comes to point to a sort of unassuming virtue, a closeness to real things which shows the behaviour of those above as un-natural and highfaluting. Being at the bottom of the ladder they have both feet on the ground. They touch basic facts, are un-protected, exposed, their vulgar ordinariness makes question-able main-plot life. Both sides stare at each other askance.

Seen from the perspective of the main plot and its intentions, of course—perspectives and intentions it is the dramatist's task to persuade his audience to endorse—these matter-of-factualists, these panders, belchers, loose livers, petty liars and lying scullions perform a number of ancillary dramatic tasks. They anchor high life to the lives of ordinary spectators or, more significantly, again, place the protagonists in a mundane and threatening perspective, as I have suggested, from which they have to be rescued. Here it is the duty of the dramatist to verify main-plot ideals against the seemingly disarming and disqualifying perspective of sub-plot comment. By surviving against this down-to-earth scepticism, high values are confirmed. A subtle and profound version of this testing occurs in Don Quixote's trials and comic tribulations, his perpetual victimization by Sancho-Panza-like facts. So, also, the sensible

Enobarbus places the divine foolishness of Antony in a cool, appraising light until he himself is overcome by Antony's magnificence. The cautious reasoning of Horatio is disqualified by Hamlet's tragic indifference and by verse within which critical perspectives wither.

On one occasion, at least, a comic sub-plot hero has attempted to elevate sub-plot realism to an equal, even superior status to the values carried by the main plot. In this extraordinary case his amazing creator tempts the values of the main plot to overcome a figure endowed with titanic comic ability and potency, with an intense and corrosive common-sense. I am thinking of Falstaff of whom, possibly, Shakespeare himself was thinking when he allows Gertrude to describe Hamlet as fat and scant of breath. Falstaff is a figure so firmly, so ostentatiously created and confirmed by his creator's gifts, so heroically equipped with an exuberant and distinguished wit that sub-plot cynicism becomes almost majestic and—while still reflecting, in a comic mirror, main-plot virtues—threatens these values themselves. He is a dramatic option not taken further, appearing again, not in the theatre, but in the pages of Nietzsche. 'Those who would be great, learn how to laugh.'

It is the main idea of these present comments that what marks out mid-twentieth century drama of the sort to which Pinter's work constitutes a distinguished part is that it has taken these sub-plot characters and left them without the main plot which gives them their dramatic rôle and place and that it is this bizarre fact with which interpretation has to work. Self-consciously you find the idea stated, if not enacted, in Stoppard's *Rosencrantz and Guildenstern are Dead*, but there the manoeuvre is a surface ploy and not part of a real, creative necessity. Intuitive and more serious and disturbing talents such as Pinter's do not aim to state the dominant idea but experience its dramatic consequences, are obliged to produce these odd works from which drama's main characters have been withheld.

Here, then, we have a world with only unrepresented values, or, rather, one in which we get only the parodied shadows of these unrealized norms, values haunting the works only through the fantasies of these abandoned sub-plot figures.

It is characteristic of Pinter's people and of sub-plot existence in general that they have no really presented psychological reality, no depth; that we should meet them and know them only through their fantasies of themselves; and that what they do should be the outcomes of a world screened by these fantasies, through a contrasting perception of squalid and demeaning states of affairs. Action itself is not the issue here since sub-plot persons do not effect change, cannot move elsewhere, are fixed to their spots. Radical drama says 'no' to this but in the world of Pinter, and his like, this is how it is. In a Pinter plot nothing good or bad comes of what is done. Again, since these are sub-plot persons how they imagine themselves constitutes a comic version of higher forms of life. They are status-seekers or rather they attribute status to themselves not so much by claiming to occupy main-plot positions but by means of the manner in which what they do and what they have been is described. For their lives are lived at the level of language; they live not by deeds but in words. They have at their disposal no power over and above the power of speech; at least, this is a dominating theme in much of his work. By its means they endow themselves with what speech can give, a language which redefines what they are in terms belonging to main-plot life. Yet they are not merely sub-plot phenomena. Since there is no main plot they come to stand for everything. Since nothing stands for an endorsed moral or normative order, since things do not and could not, here, go according to plan and yet nothing from the farcical rescues them, nothing from the tragic can touch them, we have a world of barren conversationalists, talking a life and acting it out at the level of vociferous encounters. So *The Homecoming* looks like a bitter parody of bourgeois domesticity and what the characters seem to admire they also seem to despise; life snarls at itself.

There is, however, a further aspect to Pinter's work. This is a sort of continual flirtation with the idea of something mysterious, something unsaid, something that lies beneath or outside the glittering sequences of comic chat. I think it is at this point that criticism is tempted to place Pinter's alongside the work of such as Beckett and those dramatists who consciously operate within traditions of the absurd and with notions of the unsayable which bring to mind certain twentieth-century philosophical themes and considerations. It seems to me quite wrong to try to place Pinter's work here. Pinter's silences, the moments at which the words stop, the direction of the conversation alters, the mysterious moments when odd things take place—none of this warrants taking leaves out of Wittgenstein's *Tractatus* or from the long pages of *Being and Nothingness*. In the latter case we have to do with an absurdity consequential on a lack of rational or determining reasons for choices and an incapacity of man to be other than that which acts with freedom in a world without value. None of this, it seems to me, forms part of the content of Pinter's plays. Nor is his silence the silence of which Wittgenstein speaks. There, words fail that which is not a mere matter of fact simply because meaning is associated with sentential rôle and sentential rôle with the enunciating of what is true or false. Since what is true or false—the sentence—can only be so if it pictures a mere matter of fact, what is not that—value, art, religion—can only be misrepresented by linguistic forms. What cannot be said cannot be said and that is, logically, that. Again, none of this explicates Pinter. The fact of his matter seems to be much more direct and dramatically simple. There is, of course, a sort of implicit disappointment with the ordinariness of things. This itself distinguishes it at once from Wittgenstein and the *Tractatus* where what is not able to be said is nevertheless not nothing, certainly not ordinary.

In Pinter's world, as in Mark Antony's, there is a sense of vanished music. His characters are not merely liars and imaginers: inventing a less than sordid version of what they are, they are trapped by having imaginations which never venture beyond the merely factual, artists at odds with their own drab materials, with what their own imaginations have to offer. This connects with the other aspect of his characters, at least his male characters, that they are always simmering on the edge of useless violence. Where words fail them, violence would step in, but since violence leads to nothing, they pause. Here is the simple mechanism of their lives. '. . . take a table', says Lenny in *The Homecoming*. 'Philosophically speaking. What is it?' 'A table', says his philosophical brother. G. E. Moore would have found this answer satisfactory, but it is a reply that Pinter's sub-plot fantasists find it hard to take. To be marooned in a world of sub-plot actuality and ineffectuality is what his fantasists can only endure by means of language. Other than this, there is the violence, a kind of senseless beating of heads and hearts against what is merely the case.

Take the case of the excellent *Last to Go*, a beautifully organized incident in which everything that is typical is on display and in perfect working order. A newspaper-seller stops by a drinks stand for a chat. He has sold his last one and engages the barman in apparently desultory conversation. Since all of Pinter's characters are unreformed egoists who only see from the standpoint of an intense anxiety about themselves, the conversation can only go in a direction which this total egoism demands. All conversations are contests in which self-satisfaction, or mastery, is the prize. This happens only at the level of words since, if words fail, action must ensure and that means violence. Decency, therefore—Pinter-like goodness, his character's solitary but heroic sub-plot virtue—consists in changing the subject, for, if this does not happen, they lose control. So the newspaper-seller's aim is to establish a position, score a point or two, elevate his life, make it, as it were, grand. To do this he needs to concede something to the one who is to be a witness to his small success. So he speaks to the barman as if selling drinks was more than just that—trade, it is called, and trade was, he says, very brisk a bit earlier. This is conceded by the barman and the man says he noticed.

Having done the honours and enticed the barman into conversation he goes in for a bit of inflated, nonsensical chat about what goes on when you sell your last one. Then the serious main intention emerges. Slyly, he says 'I had to go to Victoria.' His purpose, he says, was to meet George. George is somebody you have to go to Victoria to meet. 'Did you get hold of him?' asks the barman. 'No,' says the man, 'I couldn't get hold of him' and, with undermining solemnity, 'I couldn't locate him.' Then the barman tries to take George over or, rather, dispossess the man of his small prize. He says 'He's not much about much now, is he?' 'When did you last see him then?' the man says incredulously. The barman dismisses him: 'Oh, I haven't seen him for years.' The man tries to withdraw.

It is not going well. The barman now moves to occupy the field. 'Used to suffer very bad from arthritis.' 'Arthritis?' the man says, rallying. 'He never suffered from arthritis.' 'Suffered very bad.' 'Not when I knew him' is all the man can now manage. The barman closes the encounter. 'I think he must have left the area.' He has dispossessed the man of his mysterious and value-conferring friend. There is a pause. Words can do no more. They have reached a dead end and the only thing to do is to cover a retreat before things go too far. The plot of words has taken them to a point where something has to be done, to a point where something should constitute an outcome but here, in this landscape of the sub-plot, nothing happens. 'Yes', says the newspaper-seller, 'it was the Evening News was the last to go tonight.' The barman permits the retreat. 'Not always the last though, is it, though.' The newspaper man accepts a verbal, an artistic exit. 'I think he must have left the area.'

What has been looked for and lost in this unconfirmed effort? 'George?' says the barman, 'George who?' 'George', says the man, 'what's-'is-name.' George is a somebody or other who hangs around, or does not, in a lot of the plays of this period and is either a presence or an absence in a number of Pinter's. He ought to be somebody who rescues the characters from their predicaments, the main-plot person who stands for what is worthwhile. But he does not appear, like Godot or, when he does, he is not the right thing at all. In Pinter, he is not the intruder whom society wishes to expel or admit. He is much more the Chekhovian intruder of an *Uncle Vanya* sort. In the Chekhov, the household await the arrival of the professor whose career and works are to justify their otherwise trivialized lives. But when he comes he is a selfish joke, a pompous fraud. What Vanya is left with is the husk of a life. All that can be done is to go on. In Pinter the stranger, the enigmatic presence or absence, seems like an announcement of real change, of better times; he comes as if from another world, a main-plot existence. But nothing alters. Things simply continue to be banal. From the first intruder from the high life in *The Birthday Party*, the silent, senseless matchseller in *A Slight Ache* to the preposterously irresponsible Caretaker, the disappointing intruder arrives, either not a main-plot person at all or simply not able to have any effect. Even *The Homecoming* conforms to this classic pattern. The philosopher son arrives with his smart wife, stays, does nothing and leaves his wife behind and on the game.

So the small secret is out, that sub-plot men and women are stranded and without an exit because the main-plot people no longer, or never did, exist. When weeping and words and the occasional brief spasm of violence is over, so is the play. There are no messages, meanings, only the facts and those who live among them. Pinter's plays exist to contain violence and have as their primary value the ability to transform useless action into enjoyed speech. It is this which reveals the conservatism that holds his characters in place. It is the sort of conservatism which can see no way round what stares his characters in the face, the mereness of things and the fact of violence which confronts this awareness. To be more precise still, the plays exist in a sort of untragic limbo. They are devices by means of which that nothing is done is made to seem artistically satisfactory. There is great pleasure to be found in the words alone, so to represent this as a sort of barren landscape with images of failed rescue does not exactly, in the end, correspond to the psychological value of the plays. Like tragedies, they circle around domestic themes. *The Caretaker* disguises the repudiation of the father by the sons. So the themes are tragic and yet the outcomes stop far short of a tragic resolution. Indeed, their whole point is to do this. What controls the violent, tragic impulse is a sense that nothing is worthwhile and that banality can be rescued only by style. There is, also, a sense of loss, the one graceful note in a bleak, comic environment. A couple of old dears are having a cup of soup in an all-night milk-bar. Their days are organized neatly around when and where they are and when and where they eat. They talk of going down that way and going up this way and about the buses which ply these routes. It is as if they, the buses, are like galleons of light crossing the darkness. 'You'll just see the last two nine six up over the river', says one. Says the other, 'I'll just catch a look of it. Time I get up there.' There's a pause. 'It don't look like an all-night bus in the daylight do it?' It is never possible to leave well alone, nor what is ill either. Pinter's plays, like most excellent works of art, make the best of what he thinks he and it is, a world without what there once seemed to be, an inner world which, if allowed into action, would lead to what can no longer be construed tragically. Between options, all that can be done can only be done with words. When words fail, say nothing and do nothing and when this is so, the plays end. Like the end of Godot, they do not move or, rather, the conversations are at an end.

Part Two:
AN IMAGINATIVE LEAP

5

'What Have I Seen, the Scum or the Essence?': Symbolic Fallout in Pinter's *The Birthday Party*[1]

by CHARLES A. CARPENTER

> A play, once written, is something that can be approached only on its own terms—an organism that can be explored and opened up, but which can no more be tampered with or 'explained' than can any other product of nature.
>
> —Pinter, quoted by Kenneth Tynan[2]

> Astride of a grave and a difficult birth. Down in the hole, lingeringly, the grave-digger puts on the forceps.
>
> —Didi in *Waiting for Godot*

In Act II of Harold Pinter's *The Birthday Party*, Stanley Webber comes face to face with the two men whose arrival at the Boles's rooming house he had anticipated with so much dread. When he first confronts the chief intruder's bullyboy, McCann, he finds the surly Irishman seated at a table carefully tearing a sheet of newspaper into five equal strips. During the muted sparring match that follows, Webber twice picks up a strip of the paper and McCann menacingly tells him (using the same words both times), 'Mind that.' Mind it we must; symbolically or otherwise, it's got to have a point.

However, the next time McCann tears up a sheet his boss, Goldberg, notices him and comments authoritatively: 'Why do you do that all the time? It's childish, it's pointless. It's without a solitary point.' Just as emphatically, we have been conned.

Or have we? Is Pinter playing underhanded games with us—perhaps anti-symbolic games? He is, after all, the play-wright who has insisted again and again that he visualizes a concrete, particular dramatic context, one that is not even conceptual, much less symbolic; one in which the events, characters, and stage props simply *exist*.[3] He has said, 'I think there will be overtones in any work which has any kind of dimension at all . . . but there's no direct symbolic significance to anything at all that I've ever written.'[4] In fact, 'I wouldn't know a symbol if I saw one.'[5] Nevertheless, the case of McCann's 'pointless' behaviour with the newspapers cannot be dismissed simply because of Pinter's vexed disclaimers or his built-in debunker. He might *not* know a symbol if he saw one. In any event, the full range of stage business involving the papers gives them potentialities for meaning of the sort that can only be called symbolic. The beginnings of the first and third acts take place in the morning of consecutive days and include so many repetitions that a kind of treadmill effect arises. On each occasion, old Mr. Boles enters with a newspaper and reads it while his wife Meg prattles on. The process is unmistakably a ritual as regular as the daily paper itself—which, though its function is to record fluctuating reality, paradoxically fosters an illusion of stable order in a world of ceaseless change, and even supplies a brief escape from the urgent facticity of one's personal life. (As Didi remarks, 'Habit is a great deadener.') The third time Petey Boles opens a newspaper it is late in Act III, just after he has been humiliated trying to keep Stanley away from his oppressors. 'Broken' by his failure, he seeks distraction and solace in the old grooves, the fixed routines. But when he opens his most reliable escape hatch, the paper, five strips of an inside sheet flutter to the floor. Moreover, they remain on stage, mockingly radiating the destructive power and capriciousness of Goldberg and McCann, as Meg comes in to find out where Stanley is. Petey answers by ignominiously studying the front page of the paper.

What Pinter gives us here is a small theatrical bombshell with a poetic by-product, symbolic fallout. During Petey's non-striking and McCann's striking activity with the newspapers, a tiny packet of symbolic nuances is accumulated through the subtle metaphoric fabric of gesture and diction. When the curve of this sub-sub-plot reaches its apex, theatrical fireworks go off, the packet is blown open, and the nuances stream out. Some of them fall into a pattern, the recognition of which adds a distinct element of richness and pleasure to our dramatic experience. *The Birthday Party* contains several clusters of symbolically charged objects, actions, and words. These form minor patterns by themselves, and they group together to form a large, general pattern. I will tentatively call this pattern a rebirth into Hell. Often touched upon at one corner or another by critics,[6] but skirted and never examined in a concrete way, it impregnates the play to the extent that almost the entire work is an extended birthday metaphor.

Almost, but not quite. For instance, the symbolic nuances of Meg Boles asking her husband repeatedly if his newspaper is 'good', or those of McCann tearing the sheets into *five* strips, or even those of Stanley taking over the paper that Petey leaves behind in Act I, then usurping his tea, then his 'succulent' wife, cannot be forced into an all-encompassing symbolic mould without shameless sophistry. This is but to acknowledge that the symbolic fallout in Pinter's play does not violate the aesthetic imperatives of the post H-bomb world that begot it. To apply N. F. Simpson's apt phrase, it is not guilty of 'breaking faith with chaos'. The metaphorical nuances that reverberate from any basically poetic drama are surely preordained, and thus pre-ordered, to a certain indefinable degree; but a large residue—consciously engendered, purely accidental, or something in between—will inevitably remain scattered in random fashion about the play. This still chaotic residue is fully capable of reducing to absurdity all attempts to reduce it to final sense. As Pinter says,

> Meaning begins in the words, in the action, continues in your head and ends nowhere. There is no end to meaning. Meaning which is resolved, parcelled, labelled and ready for export is dead, impertinent—and meaningless.[7]

95

With this minimal apologia, I shall now proceed to tread as boldly as possible on the fallout-covered ground of *The Birthday Party*. One thing must be clear at the start, however. We are tracking down, not a symbol system or any other type of conceptual diagram, but rather the somewhat amorphously patterned symbolic overtones of a composition which is, after all, a realistic and psychological theatre piece, and only by extension a metaphorical and symbolic artwork. The play is a dynamic action or it is nothing. Mainly for this reason, when appropriate I will freely alternate and intermix the central business at hand, the metaphorical analysis of symbolically suggestive elements, with psychological interpretation of symptomatic behaviour. Simultaneously, for instance, I will speculate why Stanley resents Meg during the party (the realistic dimension) and why—blindfolded—he tries to strangle her (the symbolic one). This rather untidy process often becomes appropriate because Pinter's plays are indeed Pinteresque; the causes, motives and implications of his characters' most clear-cut gestures, though undulating with significance on stage, remain hidden in a London fog. As Pinter remarks, 'So often, below the word spoken, is the thing known and unspoken.'[8] In a diagnosis of the thing unspoken, no usable instrument is unwelcome.

One preliminary note. Some critics seem unaware that Pinter revised the original 1959 edition of the play for the 1965 Methuen and 1968 Grove Press editions, then further revised these texts for the volume entitled *Plays: One* in England (1976) and *Complete Works: One* in America (1977). As is also the case with *The Caretaker*, virtually all the revisions are cuts. Among the noteworthy passages eliminated from the first printing are two that sent McCann into the kitchen for a gratuitous salt-water gargle and brought him back, four that padded the tenuous rôle of Lulu, and three that pushed Goldberg's non-realistic side to bizarre lengths—e.g. he no longer unknowingly emits 'a high-pitched wheeze-whine'. Curiously, the first revision was a sloppy job. In the original version, Goldberg flexes his muscles on a chest expander and breaks it. This clownish bit of business is wiped out of the second version, but a vestige remains in a stage direction: McCann 'exits with the expander'. Similarly, the second edition removes the bowler hat from Stanley's hand when he appears in Act III, but Goldberg is still directed to put the hat on his victim's head when they leave. These errors, easily detectable in rehearsal, are corrected in the more recent edition.

Goldberg, prime antagonist in this natal-day play, goes by the name of Nat. His function, roughly speaking, is Nativity. Depicted as stereotypically Jewish, the key to his personality is an earnest commitment to family solidarity: 'Never, never forget your family', he says, 'for they are the rock, the constitution and the core!' The most important thing omitted from the second edition of the play is the revealing background detail (on consideration, no doubt too explicit for Pinter) that Goldberg has lost track of his only surviving son, Emanuel, who 'grew up to be a fine boy' but who left his cosy gefilte fish existence for parts unknown. Unconsciously, then, Nat craves a surrogate son. In the play he gets what he wants—or at least something like it.

What he wants, specifically, is an incarnation of his own schmaltzy ideal. Though tagged 'Emanuel', this ideal is remote from the charismatic, oracular messiah of the Bible (evoked in *The Caretaker* by the memory-image of the young Aston, before a crown of 'pincers' silenced him, talking too much about hallucinations that seemed like 'clear sight' and magnetized those he spoke to). Goldberg prefers the sheep to the shepherd. His model is the moon-faced Jesus-loves-me figure, the timid man. The first edition of the play supplies the clue: Goldberg nicknamed his own Emanuel both Manny and Timmy—thus (thus?) Timid Man. The omitted passage hammers the variant names across by comic repetition:

> McCann. I didn't know you had any sons.
> Goldberg. But of course. I've been a family man.
> McCann. How many did you have?
> Goldberg. I lost my last two—in an accident. But the first, the first grew up to be a fine boy.
> McCann. What's he doing now?
> Goldberg. I often wonder that myself. Yes. Emanuel. A quiet fellow. He never said much. Timmy I used to call him.
> McCann. Emanuel?

GOLDBERG. That's right. Manny.
McCANN. Manny?
GOLDBERG. Sure. It's short for Emanuel.
McCANN. I thought you called him Timmy.
GOLDBERG. I did.

Goldberg brings his own peculiar claim of the ideal into the scrummy, nervous home of Mr. and Mrs. Boles. Vaguely like Ibsen's Ekdals, Petey and Meg harbour their own wild-duck child, the stray pianist Stanley Webber. To put it more vulgarly than Ibsen, if not Pinter, would allow, they cherish Stanley because the Peter in their family has remained flaccid and sterile despite the symbolic come-on hidden in Meg Boles's name: she is an egg bowl (or bole—a seed receptacle; or just Margaret/Mary—a mother figure). Goldberg wants a little boy in order to regain his function as Jewish paterfamilias; Meg wants one because she is naturally maternal—instinctively 'succulent'. (When Stanley applies this term to her fried bread, she assumes it applies to herself.) Paralleling Goldberg, she envisions her son in an image shaped by her basic nature. Whereas he anticipates a carbon copy of his earlier self ('What do you think, I'm a self-made man? No! I sat where I was told to sit'), Meg asks for nothing more than an unsevered foetus, a child who accepts her protective womb and succulent breasts as his proper sphere(s) and who ventures away only as far as his prenatal leash permits.

The action of the play hinges on the conflict between these highly particularized mother- and father-figures. The two engage in a semi-conscious tug of war, with Stanley's umbilical cord as the rope, until Goldberg triumphs by virtue of superior tactics and manpower. Living up to his first name, Nat succeeds in separating the infantile Webber from an insulated web of self-indulgent womb life, and in removing him to the exposed web of moral, social and familial obligations outside. In short, he effects a forced birth. If his act is tantamount to wrenching a man from a living death and dragging him into a deathlike life (the recurring absurdist 'fall of a man from low estate'), the tragedy lies not in one set of conditions or the other, but rather in the absence of alternatives (short of actual death) in such a drastically limited world.

For Pinter's world is essentially Beckett's—one in which 'There's no lack of void', in which 'we give birth astride of a grave.' In *The Birthday Party*, Nat Goldberg is the grave-digger who puts on the forceps.

His preparations for the forced birth begin with a series of crafty ploys developed on the spot. Iago-like in his apparently motiveless malignity, Nat is also a born (and bred) opportunist. His deep compulsion to father a new plastic-age Emanuel to replace the one that spurned him, though not revealed to his consciousness, acts as the hidden dynamo behind the ceaseless revolutions of his mind. We divine this from a number of Freudian exposés and wrinkles of plot in Act I. Arriving at the Boles's house, Nat mentions his sons to McCann (in the early edition) for the first time in their long association.[9] When McCann asks about the impending job, his superior replies with his usual foggy triteness but with a note of unwitting precision: 'The main *issue* is a singular *issue*.' A few seconds after Meg discloses that it is Stanley's birthday, Goldberg leaps into control of the occasion: 'We'll give him a party. Leave it to me.' In a jot, he has planned Stanley's issuing forth, his birthday part-ing.

Other indications of the impending event have more obvious dramatic force. Stanley asks Meg both early and late in Act I why Goldberg approached Mr. Boles the night before about staying in his rooming house but did not show up until the next day. The answer is simply (in metaphorical terms) that it was not Stanley's destined birthday the night before. Also, motherly Meg, exposing her own subconscious passion for keeping her 'Stanny' close to her womb, presents him with a toy drum as a gift: that is, a membrane-covered 'piano' for the foetus to 'play on'. Stanley at first reacts with bemused indifference; but in the traumatic curtain scene, he beats the drum mechanically, then erratically, and at last wildly, 'savage and possessed'. In other words, his passive acceptance of the sordid but safe round of life within the womb-rooms provided by Meg is rapidly overcome by the terrified realization that aliens have invaded it, and he suddenly wants out. Even though there is 'nowhere' to go outside, as he has already told Lulu, 'it's no good here' any more.

In Act II, the menacers snuff out the Webber that now

exists and induce his premature rebirth. The first step involves convincing him that his present rootless, occupationless, bathless existence is actually a state of living death (which, by any reckoning, it is). Act I had amply demonstrated Stanley's reluctance to get out of bed and his propensity to collapse after doing so. Once, for example, he 'groans, his trunk falls forward, his head falls into his hands'. When Goldberg confronts him alone in Act II, he indirectly describes Stanley's condition: 'Some people don't like the idea of getting up in the morning. . . . what are you but a corpse waiting to be washed?' (Goldberg also says that rising each day ought to be more like *birth*; and Act III shows overtly that Stanley resembles a 'new man' the next morning.

With vigilant Meg busy elsewhere, Goldberg and McCann team up on Stanley in the Kafkaesque third-degree sequence, which culminates in their pronouncing him dead. Critics who have combed this amorphous verbal assault for promising specifics, such as Goldberg's 'When did you last wash up a cup?' or McCann's 'You betrayed the organization', have not satisfactorily explained the attack. Among other things, they have failed to reconcile the apparent motives of a pious English Jew with those of an avid Irish Catholic. They also seem to have undervalued the sheer 'punch' effects of dialogue, as in Goldberg's thumping, hissing speech on whether the number 846 is necessarily possible or only necessarily necessary. What Goldberg essentially does in this scene, backed by McCann, is to goad Webber's dormant sense of responsibility toward others: his 'old mum' and perhaps a fiancée he left in the lurch; an 'external force' he must acknowledge; the fellow members of his 'trade', his 'society', and his 'breed'; all the people in the Sartrean Hell of *autres* which is life outside.[10] After provoking his guilt to the point that he finally screams, the menacers consider their pre-liminary task of killing the old Webber done, and Goldberg tells him: 'You're dead. You can't live, you can't think, you can't love. You're dead. . . . You're nothing but an odour.'

He is mistaken, of course; Stanley fells him with a kick in the stomach and fends off McCann until Mrs. Boles fortuitously enters, beating the symbolic drum like a vengeful squaw. Her little boy has proven more resilient than his attackers calculated.[11] One thing Goldberg had done, for instance, was to have his muscle man disable Stanley by removing his indispensable glasses, a gesture figuratively meant to wrench him away from his womb-world—to 'impose . . . upon the room/ A dislocation and doom', as Pinter expresses it in his poem about the play, 'A View of the Party'.[12] With Meg present, however, Stanley is able to restore his former vision of that world simply by asking to have his glasses back. Although he is so beaten down that these are his last words in the play onstage (offstage, he apparently babbles much of the night), his oppressors must clearly take more conclusive measures.

It is during the birthday party itself that Goldberg succeeds in engineering Webber's phoenix-like metamorphosis. He 'finishes him off' in two subtle stages. The first occurs during the ostensibly cheerful toasting of Stanley, and serves to counteract possessive Meg's presence. Setting a third-degree atmosphere by ordering McCann to darken the room and shine a flashlight on 'the birthday boy' (while Meg is vainly claiming 'he's my Stanley now'), Goldberg nudges Webber back into the frame of mind that was so effectively imposed upon him just before Meg arrived, an acute awareness of the Hell of other people. The second stage is signalled when McCann, cued by his boss, sings the pointed line, 'the Garden of Eden has vanished'.[13] The Boles's home is Stanley's Eden (a garden path leads to the front door). Ironically, it is the proprietress of this mixed-blessing sanctuary, Meg, who teases him to play blind-man's buff and covers his eyes with a scarf. Still, it is the dutiful stooge McCann who appropriates his glasses and snaps their frames, ending his comfortable image of womb-life forever. (In Act III Goldberg will not let Petey tape up his glasses, and he tells Webber outright that they had made him 'cockeyed'.) The last lines of Pinter's 'A View of the Party' refer poignantly to 'Stanley's final eyes/ Broken by McCann'.

Nat Goldberg's keenly intuitive, if not rationally formulated machinations reduce Stanley to a set of random twitches. The key death-twitch is a birth tremor. Symbolically, the old Webber will remain intact and the new Webber unborn until Meg's proudly offered gift, the drum-womb, is broken; therefore McCann places the drum where the blinded Stanley will step into it.[14] What follows has been consistently misinterpreted. With his blindfold still secure, Stanley punctures the drum with his foot (improbably, since the drum is on its side and he is walking slowly) and falls down. Quite non-realistically, he rises without removing the drum from his foot or the blindfold from his eyes. Then he drags himself over to Meg, 'reaches her and stops. His hands move towards her and they reach her throat [though he cannot see a thing]. He begins to strangle her.' Commentators on the play have ignored the symbolic implications of this sequence, though it radiates them like a surrealist melodrama. (Indeed, even those critics who view the scene as realism skewed by psychosis forget that Stanley cannot *see* the person he is choking.[15]) Stanley's actions here can be accounted for, but perhaps only in terms of the symbolic birthday metaphor that infuses the play.

From his point of view, Meg has betrayed him. Formerly a repugnant but always solicitous mother-substitute (just old enough to be his mother, in fact), and symbolically a 'succulent old washing bag [bag of waters]', she has unwittingly misled him into believing that she is ready to expel her cherished foetus. First, against his wishes she revealed the date of his birth (he denies it repeatedly, but she may be right; what matters is that she established the premise upon which others act). This of course opened the door for the fatal birthday party. Second, despite her insistence during the toast that she is 'so happy, having him here and not gone away, on his birthday', she let down her guard by drinking too much liquor when he was more dependent than ever on her protection. This was actually McCann's doing; part of his obstetrical assignment was to ply the mother with anaesthetizing whisky. But all Stanley saw was a giddy, booze-swilling creature playing up to an ominous bully somewhat younger than himself—and, for the moment, much more fascinating to Meg. Finally, Meg encouraged the climactic game of blind man's buff, stood by and said nothing when McCann broke Stanley's glasses and placed the drum in his path, and reacted with only an ambiguous 'Ooh!' when he rent the crucial drum-skin. Responding unconsciously to these stimuli, he carries out the symbolic action of trying to strangle the old woman. Suppressed, he mutely conveys the focus of his rage a second later by giving 'a sharp, sustained rat-a-tat with a stick on the side of the drum'.

The astonishing final events in Act II have fared no better at the hands of critics. In almost total darkness, 'Lulu suddenly perceives [Stanley] moving towards her, screams and faints.' He picks her up, places her 'spread-eagled' on a table, and is soon discovered 'bent over her'. Virtually every commentator on *The Birthday Party*, from the casual to the cumbersome, has dismissed this as an attempted rape. Perhaps disarmed by the similar occurrence in Ionesco's *The Lesson*—a knife-murder which is undeniably a symbolic rape, and which also displays the girl spread-eagled on a table— these critics have remained oblivious to the plain fact that Stanley has moved Lulu from an advantageous raping position, flat on the floor, to an impossible one (barring a unique expertise at table-raping). The fact is that he does not have sex on his mind at all. Unconsciously, as revealed by this further step in his recent series of symbolic activities, he seeks a new source of the Edenic womb-life he has lost. Meg has failed him; perhaps Lulu will not. It was she, after all, who brought the drum originally. In the blackness, Stanley weirdly and ritualistically 'measures' Lulu for the rôle of Mother.[16]

The glare of McCann's flashlight ends his desperate flight of wishful thinking, however, and exposes him as the naked, wellnigh helpless babe that he now is. Webber has been forcibly returned to the world he had inadvertently defined by telling McCann that he was born and brought up near Maidenhead, an area in which the portals of womb-Edens would all be closed off. This is also the world of the trite, hypocritical, solid-citizen Goldbergs. If 'Stan' is not literally 'Nat's' (except backwards), at least both are known to have spent much time in Basingstoke, a venerable town steeped in tradition but sacrificed to commercialization; and both recall a Boots' rental library and a Fuller's teashop, bastions of banal respectability with outlets all over England in the 1950s. Webber knows this generalized society-Hell all too intimately. Therefore he reacts to his forced rebirth into it—and brings down the curtain—by uncontrollably giggling. In much the same manner as he had played the drum at the end of the previous act, he strangely begins giggling the instant McCann's light hits him, then giggles more and more hysterically as Goldberg and his bullyboy close in. Stanley's reaction, symbolically conveying his foreknowledge of life 'near Maidenhead', has the touch of utter appropriateness. In necessarily preliterate, babyish terms, his giggling intensely communicates not only the expected pangs of terror, but also a knife-edge sensation of absurdity.

It is no coincidence that the two 'peak emotions' in *The Birthday Party*, terror and absurdity, are wholly characteristic of the theatre of the absurd. Pinter is very much one of Beckett's fellow travellers.[17] However, he is also proficient enough in the reactionary art of that West End staple, the well-made play, to adapt its time-worn formula to his own ends. In good expository fashion—though lacking the usual spate of solid background data—Act I of *The Birthday Party* systematically introduces the opposing agents who will participate in the play's main conflict, the competition between Meg and Nat for Stanley. The dynamics of character interplay derive chiefly from a subtle variation of the eternal triangle (a Pinter as well as Pinero favourite: witness *The Room*, *A Slight Ache*, *The Collection*, *The Basement*, *Silence*, *Old Times*, and *Betrayal*). The first act also develops the play's chief suspense-builder: the secret of why Goldberg has come. Artifice showing to the extent of parody, Pinter rigs an improbable moment of privacy in the Boles's living room for McCann to question his boss about the job at hand. Goldberg's long reply—'The main issue is a singular issue. . . . Certain elements, however, might well approximate in points of procedure to some of your other activities', etc.—is a classic example of the deliberately frustrating say-nothing dodge.[18] Act II carries the conflict forward to its climax through an adeptly contrived pattern of rising action. Stanley confronts the stooge McCann, then the 'top banana' Goldberg, then both of the conspirators, until at last Meg and Lulu arrive for the *scène à faire*. The ensuing climax tidily combines a discovery—of the secret about Goldberg's presence—and a reversal—of Stanley's fortunes. As far as the plot is concerned, the play is virtually over except for a few explanations of what happened and why; and Act III consists largely of people telling each other just that (obliquely, to be sure). The leftover falling action merely creates enough stage movement to group and regroup the characters conveniently.

Pinter fits the more innovative dimension of the play, its extended birthday metaphor, into this well-made mould. The expository act establishes the metaphoric terms of the 'real' undercover conflict, from the time Meg hears that Lady Mary Splatt had a baby girl and remarks, 'I'd much rather have a little boy', to Goldberg's prophetic vow to cheer Webber up: 'We'll bring him out of himself.' The key symbol, the toy drum, is of course featured in the act. After the gradual build-up in Act II, the climax reached, metaphorically viewed, is Stanley's simultaneous death and rebirth. Before this, his glasses are the symbolic focal point, with related blinding and illuminating devices (like the torch, which is both) clustered around.[19] All that Act III must accomplish in these terms is an explanation of what happened and why. The fact that none of the characters could possibly understand, much less articulate, what happened on this metaphoric level no doubt raised difficulties for Pinter; but it did not stop the virtuoso of sub-textual reference, double entendre and allusion from communicating what was vital.

He naturally assigned most of the undercover explaining to his chief obstetrician, Goldberg. Called Benny by his father and Simey by his mother and wife, Goldberg insists that his natal assistant McCann call him Nat. Unconsciously, he knows his function. Asked by Mr. Boles what came over Stanley at the party, Goldberg responds with his usual surface fogginess, but the import of his words is accessible enough: 'What came over him? Breakdown, Mr. Boles. Pure and simple.' His allusion to the broken symbolic drum, and through that to Stanley's exit from the womb, is hard to miss: a few moments before, Meg had picked up the drum and referred to it as 'broken' four times. Her husband next asks Goldberg what brought on the breakdown so suddenly. 'It can happen in all sorts of ways', Nat replies; and his specific example of a sudden (nervous) breakdown evokes the case of Stanley's forced premature birth almost inescapably:

sometimes it happens gradual—day by day it grows and grows.
. . . And then other times it happens all at once. Poof! Like that!
The nerves break. There's no guarantee how it's going to
happen, but with certain people . . . it's a foregone conclusion.

Nat should know. Mr. Boles gets in on the unconscious
allusion game himself with part of his next question: 'they can
recover [re-cover] from it, can't they?' Here as elsewhere,
insistent repetitions in the dialogue compel our attention to
veiled meanings:

> GOLDBERG. Recover? Yes, sometimes they recover, in one way
> or another.
> PETEY. I mean, he might have recovered by now, mightn't he?
> GOLDBERG. It's conceivable. Conceivable.

Translated, the premature baby might indeed get re-covered;
the 'one way or another' would be to be re-conceived. Petey
has already suggested to Meg that she might obtain another
drum for Stanley, the symbolic equivalent of reconception.
However, he cannot singlehandedly prevent Goldberg from
taking Stanley away, and Meg herself—ignorant of Stanley's
condition because she drank too much at the party—does not
even stay around to bolster the resistance.

Goldberg also explains in the course of Act III why the
birthday party took place. First to McCann, then to Webber,
he obliquely describes the world his newly adopted, soon-to-
be-readapted son will enjoy when he gets his new glasses. By
nature, it is a static world, atrophied at the stage of mental
infancy. Nat boasts openly to McCann of being fit as a fiddle
because he followed the line, played the game, and never
forgot his family; but concealed in his Polonian blather is a
hint of the more fundamental reason: 'I've never lost a tooth.
Not since the day I was born[!]. Nothing's changed.' The most
revealing statement Goldberg makes about his world is the
least voluntary one. Groping for a rationale to substantiate his
follow-the-line, play-the-game ethic, he slips into a deadly
serious caricature of existential *Angst*:

> And you'll find—that what I say is true.
> Because I believe that the world . . . (*Vacant.*). . . .
> Because I believe that the world . . . (*Desperate.*). . . .
> BECAUSE I BELIEVE THAT THE WORLD . . . (*Lost.*). . . .

Shaken to his soul, Goldberg recovers his aplomb by having McCann (allegedly a defrocked priest) blow air in his mouth. His performance is clearly another caricature, this time an inane one of the popular Eastern alternative to Western nihilism, Hindu spirituality. The sham yogi tops off his effort to restore the tranquillity of his spirit through the breath of life by asking McCann to give him 'One for the road'.

Talking to Stanley about the prospect that faces him now that he is 'a new man', Nat again paints the surface of his world with conventional virtues—discounts, medicaid, regular exercise and church attendance, a sure ladder to success—but again, seconded by McCann, he accidentally conveys the true nature of that world. 'You need a long convalescence', Goldberg says to Stanley.

> McCANN. Where angels fear to tread.
> GOLDBERG. Exactly.

Stanley's new life will be—a long wait in Hell. Later the two make it apparent that if Stanley will submit himself to the control of a paternalistic authority such as Nat, he will soon become 'adjusted', 'reorientated', 'integrated'—in effect, a completely subordinated child. Goldberg agrees to provide him not only with hot tips and ear plugs, but also with baby powder, 'day and night service' (for dirty nappies?), and a skipping rope; and he finally calls him 'Stanny boy', Meg's pet words for him. McCann adds, 'You'll be our pride and joy.' The quashed but wriggling Stanley, pressed for his opinion of the prospect, conveys his nausea by forcing out the same sound two different times: 'Caahh . . . caahh.' In many countries, 'caca' (from the Greek root *kakka*-) is 'shit' in little boy's language. Stanley not only says it twice, but Pinter's stage directions can be construed to put him through the motions of defecating, baby fashion. Seated in a chair, he 'concentrates' and 'crouches', then emits grunting sounds. After a moment, 'his chin draws into his chest'—that is, he looks down at his pants—and his body 'shudders'.[20]

Stanley's profanity is his last rebellious gesture. The remnant of action in the play serves to confirm the nature of his transformation and to settle his immediate destiny. The new baby boy, cleaned up as well as brainwashed by the two obstetricians

107

during the night after the party, is as prepared as he ever will be to accept what is coming: 'special treatment' at the hands of 'Monty'. Symbolically, Monty might represent the mountain peak of Goldberg's world, his own family (which he refers to as 'the rock'). Nat describes Monty simply as 'the best there is', and to him the best mountain there is would of course be a gold berg. Several critics have asserted that Stanley is being taken away—at least in a figurative sense—to his own funeral. He is dressed in coffin clothes, they note, and he is about to be driven off in a 'big car' whose 'beautiful boot' has 'just room . . . for the right amount'. Besides, in Act I Goldberg has remarked to McCann, 'Everywhere you go these days it's like a funeral.' The trouble with this theory is that the evidence offered to support it actually rules it out. In the first edition of the play, Stanley is clad in striped trousers and a black jacket, and he carries a bowler hat. The hat should be enough to keep a corpse-in-a-coffin image from growing in our minds, especially when it is placed on his head. The revised edition omits the hat but changes Stanley's image into a duplicate of Goldberg's; he merely wears a 'dark well cut suit'. If his own garb is funereal, so is the undertaker's. More reasonably, we are to perceive that Stanley has made a forced re-entry into Goldberg's world. As for the hearse-like car, its cherished boot does not imply that the car might very well be a hearse, but that it cannot be one. A 'boot' is a trunk, and hearses do not have trunks. Besides, Pinter excised this ominously reverberating line from the latest edition of the play and substituted the bland 'There's room there. Room in the front, and room in the back.'

More seriously off base than these niggling specifics, however, is the general idea that Stanley Webber has been turned into a corpse, a vegetable, or something else devoid of active nerve endings. On the contrary, this is the state he had groped for in Meg's womb-rooms and has now lost. Paralleling Job before his own thunderous, irrational intimidation, Stanley wishes he had never been born. Like so many existentialist anti-heroes struck by the insufferable absurdity of a life analogous to a grade-B version of the ordeal of Sisyphus, he shares the dream of Beckett's Clov, who craves the perfect order of a world 'silent and still . . . under the last dust'.

Stanley had even acted in accord with such convictions, focusing his energies on staying in bed as long as possible. Now, having been kept up all night, he is far from dead or senseless. His last sound is not a death rattle but a writhing child's obscenity. Mr. Boles's parting words to him are not 'Rest in peace in your new home', but rather 'Don't let them tell you what to do.' When the old man is left alone and Meg appears after a trip to the store, she comments that it is hot outside—in the Hell which Stanley has re-entered. When she asks about Stanley, Petey conceals his shame behind the daily paper, then unwittingly exposes it in the form of an empathetic wish, lying to her that Stanley is asleep. Again reflecting his lost ward's fondest pipedream, he adds: 'Let him . . . sleep.' Meg, thoroughly deceived, bubbles out her notes of tragic irony with a vibrato of absurdity:

> MEG. Wasn't it a lovely party last night?
> PETEY. I wasn't there.
> MEG. Weren't you?
> PETEY. I came in afterwards.
> MEG. Oh. (*Pause*) It was a lovely party.

'You can make symbolic meat out of anything', the creator of Meg's lovely party has warned. He has also said: 'The most we know for sure is that the things which have happened have happened in a certain order: any connections we think we see, or choose to make, are pure guesswork.' In his radio play, *The Dwarfs*, a character broods about his fragmented image of a friend and asks himself, 'What have I seen, the scum or the essence?' The symbol-hunter in Pinterland would do well to apply this question to himself—and to bear in mind that fallout of any type is more akin to scum than to essence.

NOTES

1. In slightly different form, this article first appeared in *Modern Drama*, 17, 1974, 389–402, and is reprinted by permission of the editor, Jill Levenson. The reception of the essay over the years has convinced me that the sceptical colouring I had given it is far too easy to ignore or shrug off. Yet a major point of the essay is that a critical reading of a Pinter play

must be essentially speculative and inconclusive. This updated version therefore includes, not only further documentation of my argument, but also several 'counter-notes' designed explicitly to undermine some of its shakier props—leaving them, in the mode of Derrida, 'legible yet effaced'. Pinter has further encouraged this sort of interpretive scepticism by releasing a letter about *The Birthday Party* that he wrote to Peter Wood, director of the first production, before rehearsals began in early 1958. Wood had apparently urged him to 'insert a clarification or moral judgement or author's angle' in the play (or at least in a programme note). But Pinter insisted: 'The curtain goes up and comes down. Something has happened. Right? Cockeyed, brutish, absurd, with no comment. Where is the comment, the slant, the explanatory note? In the play. Everything to do with the play is in the play' ('A Letter to Peter Wood', printed in *Drama*, No. 142, 1981, pp. 4–5, and in *Kenyon Review*, 3, iii, 1981, 2–5).

2. From an interview quoted in Edward R. H. Malpas, 'A Critical Analysis of the Stage Plays of Harold Pinter', unpublished dissertation, University of Wisconsin, 1965, p. 85.

3. See especially 'Writing for the Theatre' in Pinter's *Plays: One* (London: Eyre Methuen, 1976), pp. 10–11, and Lawrence M. Bensky, 'Harold Pinter: An Interview', *Paris Review*, No. 10, 1966, p. 24.

4. From a 1960 B.B.C. Television interview quoted in Kay Dick, 'Mr. Pinter and the Fearful Matter', *Texas Quarterly*, 4, 1961, 264.

5. 'Writing for Myself' in Pinter's *Plays: Two* (London: Eyre Methuen, 1977), p. 10.

6. The most rich and suggestive studies of the play are the sections on it in the books about Pinter by Katherine H. Burkman, Bernard F. Dukore, Martin Esslin, Lucina P. Gabbard, Steven H. Gale, Rüdiger Imhof, and Daniel Salem, and the following essays: John Ditsky, 'Pinter's Christ of Complicity: *The Birthday Party*', in his *The Onstage Christ* (London: Vision, 1980), pp. 136–46; Robert B. Heilman, 'Demonic Strategies: *The Birthday Party* and *The Firebugs*', in Brom Weber (ed.), *Sense and Sensibility in Twentieth-Century Writing* (Carbondale: Southern Illinois University Press, 1970), pp. 57–74; Michael W. Kaufman, 'Actions That a Man Might Play: Pinter's *The Birthday Party*', *Modern Drama*, 16, 1973, 167–78; Simon O. Lesser, 'Reflections on Pinter's *The Birthday Party*', *Contemporary Literature*, 13, 1972, 34–43, reprinted in his *The Whispered Meanings* (Amherst: University of Massachusetts Press, 1977), pp. 203–11; Rudolf Stamm, 'Geburtstag in T. S. Eliots *The Family Reunion* und Harold Pinters *The Birthday Party*', in Claus Uhlig and Volker Bischoff (eds.), *Die amerikanische Literatur in der Weltliteratur* (Berlin: Schmidt, 1982), pp. 323–38; and Heinz Zimmerman, 'Harold Pinter: *The Birthday Party*', in Klaus D. Fehse and Norbert Platz (eds.), *Das zeitgenössische englische Drama* (Frankfurt: Athenäum, 1975), pp. 43–70; see also notes 12 and 19.

7. 'A Letter to Peter Wood'.

8. 'Writing for the Theatre', p. 13.

9. The effect of the revised version, however, is the opposite: Goldberg still

tells McCann that on business trips 'One of my sons used to come with me', but McCann does not respond to the comment at all; i.e. he acts as if he had heard of the sons before.

10. In his recently published 1958 letter on the play, Pinter interprets this main line of action as follows: 'the hierarchy, the Establishment, the arbiters, the socio-religious monsters arrive to effect alteration and censure upon a member of the club who has discarded responsibility . . . towards himself and others. . . . he collapses under the weight of their accusation—an accusation compounded of the shitstained strictures of centuries of "tradition" ' ('A Letter to Peter Wood').

11. Pinter's 1958 letter puts surprising emphasis on the fact that Stanley 'fights for his life', which shows he has 'a certain fibre'. He loses miserably because 'he is not *articulate*. . . . Stanley *cannot* perceive his only valid justification—which is he is what he is—therefore he certainly can never be articulate about it. He knows only to attempt to justify himself by dream, by pretence and by bluff, through fright. If he had cottoned on to the fact that he need only admit to himself what he actually is and is not—then Goldberg and McCann would not have paid their visit, or if they had, the same course of events would have been by no means assured' ('A Letter to Peter Wood').

12. The poem, first published in 1958, is printed by Pinter, *Poems and Prose, 1949–1977* (New York: Grove Press, 1978). Andreas Fischer discusses the poem in relation to the play very provocatively in 'Poetry and Drama: Pinter's Play *The Birthday Party* in the light of his poem "A View of the Party" ', *English Studies*, 60, 1979, 484–97.

13. In context, the impact of this line may tend in the opposite direction:

> Oh, the Garden of Eden has vanished, they say,
> But I know the lie of it still.
> Just turn to the left at the foot of Ben Clay
> And stop when halfway to Coote Hill.
> It's there you will find it, I know sure enough. . . .

14. A problem in staging this action exposes a problem in my interpretation of the drum. As Stanley moves 'very slowly', McCann places the drum 'sideways' in his path. 'Stanley walks into the drum and falls over with his foot caught in it.' How is this staged? Surely the actor cannot kick out suddenly to puncture the drum; but short of doing that, his foot would rebound and the drum bounce or roll away. He would have an especially difficult job penetrating a drum covered with stretched skin—i.e. a womb-like drum. Moreover, breaking into a drum is hardly analogous to breaking out of a womb; the action might indeed suggest the idea to a literary analyst, but it would almost surely not evoke the image for a spectator.

15. However, he might well have located Meg orally when she cried 'Ooh!' Alternatively, he might have intended to strangle Goldberg or McCann, but happened upon Meg instead.

16. I can offer only a counter-feeling, not a counter-note, to this interpretation: it seems ingenious to the point of absurdity.

17. At least until recently. On 18 January 1984, Pinter was interviewed on British television by Channel Four News after participating in a programme at The Pit, Barbican, entitled 'Unpersons'. Asked why he associated himself with an occasion for political protest, Pinter replied: 'Because I think I, in common with a great body of people, have been sleepwalking for many years. . . . Years ago I regarded myself as an artist in an ivory tower—when it came down to it, a rather classic nineteenth-century idea. I've now totally rejected that. . . . I find that the things that [are] actually happening are not only of the greatest importance but have a most crucial bearing on our lives.'

18. Just before this Pinter has toyed cutely with our desire to know who Goldberg is:

> GOLDBERG. . . . You're a capable man, McCann.
> McCANN. That's a great compliment, Nat, coming from a man in your position.
> GOLDBERG. Well, I've got a position, I won't deny it.
> McCANN. You certainly have.
> GOLDBERG. I would never deny that I had a position.
> McCANN. And what a position!
> GOLDBERG. It's not a thing I would deny.

19. For extended treatments of the sight imagery, see Peter C. Thornton, 'Blindness and the Confrontation with Death: Three Plays by Harold Pinter', *Die Neueren Sprachen*, 17, 1968, 213–23, and Ann P. Messenger, 'Blindness and the Problem of Identity in Pinter's Plays', *Die Neueren Sprachen*, 21, 1972, 481–90.

20. This interpretation is partly playful, of course, but Pinter may actually have had the idea in mind; his 1958 letter says that 'In the third act Stanley can do nothing but make a noise. . . . He is trying to go further. He is on the edge of utterance. But it's a long, impossible edge and utterance, were he to succeed in falling into it, might very well prove to be only one cataclysmic, profound fart' ('A Letter to Peter Wood').

6

Names and Naming in the Plays of Harold Pinter

by RONALD KNOWLES

In 1978 it was reported that Harold Pinter had withdrawn 200 production typescripts of *Betrayal* because the characters' names had not been centred, but appeared at the side of the scripts, which subsequently had to be retyped.[1] Though this might appear capricious it will be shown that the alteration is fundamental to Pinter's writing. It is true that in the publication of Pinter's plays since *Landscape* and *Silence* names had been centred. But Pinter's action was not simply to ensure uniformity. No dramatist has been so consistently and conspicuously concerned with names and naming throughout his career. It is hoped that critical recognition of this will add to a more precise understanding of Pinter's work.

This essay will examine the principal categories of names and naming, including such issues as social and existential identity, and the instrumentality of naming in the exercise of power. A section is devoted to Pinter's use of naming in the structure of the plays; essentially, if drama consists of encounter and confrontation within the opening and closing of act and work, then, as will be demonstrated, names and naming contribute intrinsically to the design of each play as a whole.[2] Given the focus of this essay, the question of mannerism has to be raised and is put in relation to *No Man's Land*. The close of the essay will turn to three different categories of names and naming: those who are present on stage but who remain unnamed in the course of the play; those who are absent but are given a kind of presence by being named onstage; the function of the names of places and pubs. Consideration of these topics gives rise to a possible overview of Pinter's work in terms of the relationship between his distinctive dramatic 'alienation effect' and social alienation itself. This entails discussion of speech, identity and what I term 'tangency of being'. In conclusion an attempt will be made to place Pinter as a particular kind of existential writer.

In *The Room*, the blind negro Riley, rising from the blackness of the basement and entering Rose's room with the darkness of night, is vulnerable, incapacitated and alien—and yet the bearer of identity. 'Come home, Sal' (I. 124) he repeats on behalf of Rose's father. Rose's putative security has been undermined by Bert's dumbness, Mr. Kidd's seeming deafness and now by Riley's blindness—'You're all deaf and dumb and blind, the lot of you . . .' (I. 123), she says. The movement of the play reveals Rose's inability to recognize the nature of her being. She is forced to recognize a truer identity. Her identity as 'Rose' or 'Mrs. Hudd' is a kind of negation which culminates in her reply '. . . I don't know you and nobody knows I'm here and I don't know anybody anyway' (I. 124). The nullity of her isolation is first seen in the way she ministers to Bert's silent domination. Rose's remark 'That's right. You eat that . . .' (I. 101), *following* the cue stage direction 'BERT *begins to eat*', indicates her larger situation. Her remarks follow his actions making what otherwise appear unreflective responses into a kind of directive, as if she were the instigator of her situation and Bert the acquiescent agent, instead of the reverse. Rose's insistent praise of the relative comforts of the room both keeps silence at bay and forestalls any reflection on what she really feels about her situation. Mr. Sands's later remark '. . . Must be lonely for you, being all alone here . . .' (I. 118) gives voice to the truth behind her apparent concern about Bert's departure. A silent presence is better than the presence of silence. '. . . We keep ourselves to ourselves . . .' Rose says (I. 115), but self-confrontation is effectively minimized by the empty reassurance of 'we . . . ourselves'. Rose sustains herself by the repeated comparison with the basement, i.e. with what and where she is not, rather than what and where she is. The visitors to the room cumulatively anticipate Rose's disorientation in terms of names and identity.

Since Mr. Kidd is not entirely sure whether his mother was Jewish or not, his own social identity is brought into question. Again, the Sands' upper-class forenames—'Toddy' and 'Clarissa'—are quite at odds with their lower-class speech. Rose herself flatly refuses to believe that 'Riley' is the negro's real name. Yet Rose recognizes an affinity with him. Riley, a blind negro bearing a father's request and another name, paradoxically embodies the foreign in the familiar, the symbol of Rose's existential identity, an identity conferred by existence itself, and what it has added up to, not by parents. Amidst the seemingly secure, comfortable and familiar, this middle-aged woman is ultimately estranged, fearful and alien. Stanley Webber in *The Birthday Party* undergoes a comparable experience.

'Webber! Why did you change your name?' (I.60) is part of Goldberg and McCann's extensive interrogation. Whatever the past truth, the name 'Stanley Webber' identifies the present life of seedy retreat led by this indolent lodger in a seaside boarding house. After his breakdown Stanley is reduced to a speechless cypher of surface respectability, his real identity quite lost. In *The Birthday Party* Pinter dramatizes the way in which first names are used by an individual or others to protect or negotiate versions of self. Meg's maternal possessiveness is expressed by the diminutive 'Stanny'. Her version of Stanley is of a boy who needs mothering, or as someone to flirt with. Clearly paralleling this is Nat Goldberg's sentimental recall of the wife and mother to whom he was 'Simey', an exclusive aspect of his past identity which he jealously guards, rejecting McCann's appropriation with 'NEVER CALL ME THAT' (I. 86). Alternatively, to his father the young Goldberg was 'Benny'. Goldberg reassures Petey after Stanley's collapse by introducing McCann's first name, 'Anyway, Dermot's with him at the moment. He's . . . keeping him company' (I. 81). Goldberg thereby extends the intimacy of friendship suggesting the help of close well-wishers rather than the tormentors that he and McCann actually are. The same tactic is turned on McCann himself, '. . . And I knew the word I had to remember—Respect! Because

115

McCann—(*Gently*). Seamus—who came before your father?'
(I. 88). In spite of the stage direction '*Gently*' this demonstrates
the measure of Goldberg's power over McCann; he does what
he has just rebuked McCann for doing. Access to intimacy by
the familiar usage of a first name clearly fascinates Pinter.

Miss Cutts, in *The Hothouse*, provokes Roote, her lover, by
wearing the negligee of a patient (on whom he has fathered a
child) and recounting their conversation:

> She's so sweet, and she's got such a bonny baby. I said to her,
> now we're friends, I can't go on calling you 6459, can I? What's
> your name? Do you know, she wouldn't tell me? Well, what
> does your lover call you? I said, what little nickname? She
> blushed to the roots of her hair. I must say I'm very curious.
> What could he have called her? She's sweet, but she said the
> baby misses his Daddy. Babies do miss Daddy, you know.
> Archie, can't the baby see his Daddy, just for a little while, just
> to say hello? (p. 140)

It is as if knowledge and the use of a name form is a kind of
articulated power. Miss Cutts indirectly declares her superi-
ority over her rival by using the familiar version of Roote's
christian name for the first and only time here, towards the
close of the play. She is reappropriating her lover by reappropriating the name in evoking and triumphing over the
rival situation. Similarly, James is Jimmy to his wife in *The
Collection*, whereas to Harry on first meeting he is 'Mr. Horne'
(II.153), and then the bluff, clubby 'Horne' (II. 155). However, in attempting to prevent Bill's final confession, Harry
tries to encourage James's departure, completing the pro-
gression from formality to familiarity: 'Come on, Jimmy, I
think we've had enough of this stupidity don't you?' (II. 156).
The possibility of this being a slip rather than a calculated
overture keeps open the option of retrieving a position. Harry
has just urged Bill 'Come on, Billy, I think we've had enough
of this stupidity, don't you?' (II. 156), which implies a parallel
relationship, thus including James in the homosexual ambience
of the household, an ambience he has in fact courted by his
behaviour with Bill. Harry evidently has some doubts about
James's sexual orientation and the 'slip' into the familiar form
obliquely tests this, but James immediately picks up the

implication and quickly rebuffs him by a gesture—'JAMES *looks at him sharply*' (II. 156).

This proprietorial naming is what Edward resists in *A Slight Ache*. 'And stop calling me Edward' (I. 189) he vainly orders Flora, much as he has objected to her self-consciously childish endearment 'Oh, Weddie. Beddie-Weddie. . . .' 'Do not call me that' (I. 178). When Edward is finally displaced by the matchseller, as we might expect he is displaced in name as well. Having dwelt on the day as the longest of the year, Flora aptly names the newcomer after the appropriate saint: 'I am going to keep you, you dreadful chap, and call you Barnabas' (I. 192).[3] This naming is a form of possession, unlike that of Pinter's most famous play where power is exercised by naming as a form of rejection.

Bernard Jenkins, we recall, is the assumed name of Mac Davies, the tramp in *The Caretaker*. 'Papers' proving his real identity have been left at Sidcup 'about near on fifteen year ago' (II. 30). Pinter works on several levels here. These distant papers furnish Davies with a permanent excuse for his seemingly provisional evasiveness, thereby adding a specific comic dimension to his prevarication. Yet, at the same time, we are made aware of the gap between bureaucratic and existential identity. Davies is at the opposite remove to characters like Goldberg and Roote. They have relative power and authority deriving from an unspecified bureaucracy. 'Jenkins' is powerless but notionally pursues the idea of finding a legitimate bureaucratic identity as a restored Mac Davies, on the right side of authority, complete with papers: 'They prove who I am. . . . They tell you who I am' (II. 29). But Davies' existential identity is manifestly there before us in all its uncompromising starkness. Davies is what he has become—that existential imbalance between what he has made of life and what life has made of him. Mick instinctively recognizes the disjunction between these identities and plays on Davies's need for some kind of social legitimacy: 'Who do you bank with?' (II. 45). From the outset he has repeatedly put his finger on Davies's most vulnerable point—'Jen . . . kins' (II. 39, 42)—and at the close he works through his strategy of rejection (II. 81–2):

117

MICK. What is your name?
DAVIES. Don't start that—
MICK. No, what's your real name?
DAVIES. My real name's Davies.
MICK. What's the name you go under?
DAVIES. Jenkins!

In reality the struggle between Mick and Davies had been one-sided; Davies only continued in the attic on sufferance. In contrast, the contest between Lenny and Ruth in *The Homecoming* ends in a kind of truce. On first encounter, Ruth, like Mick, successfully uses the probe of a name. In spite of Lenny's graphically extended verbal assaults, Ruth instinctively undermines him by anticipating part of a compound rôle. Lenny insists that she has drunk enough water:

LENNY. Quite sufficient, in my opinion.
RUTH. Not in mine, Leonard.

> *Pause*

LENNY. Don't call me that, please.
RUTH. Why not?
LENNY. That's the name my mother gave me. (III. 49)

Lenny only glimpses the larger psychological implications of this admission and continues his attempt to dominate. Ruth's combination of maternal and openly aggressive stances prove too much for Lenny who shows signs of losing control in near panic.

However, what makes *The Homecoming* unique in terms of Pinter's naming is not so much the use of first names or surnames as words denoting family relationship throughout the whole play. We find primarily family, dad, father, mother, mum, son, brother, wife, uncle, and secondarily sister-in-law, brother-in-law, daughter-in-law, nephews, grandchildren, grandfather. These words occur approximately 130 times in the play. 'But nevertheless we do make up a unit', Lenny tells Teddy, 'and you're an integral part of it' (II. 81). The focus here is on the need for the mutuality of familial identity, each individual subsumed by the compound identity of the family, represented by Max, its vituperative patriarch. Yet in speech and action every family relationship is mocked or scorned. Pinter dramatizes this by clustering these familial terms for powerful ironic effect. They are not simply diffused within the play. For example, when Teddy refuses to contribute money to support Ruth in the London household, Max retorts 'What? You won't even help to support your own wife? I thought he was a son of mine. You lousy stinkpig. Your mother would drop dead if she heard you taking that attitude' (III. 87).[4] It would seem as if instead of the binding power of love, care and respect, we find an habituated hostility which degrades what comes in contact with it, in a travesty of family values. Yet, apart from Teddy, the family has remained together in a kind of atavistic bond, and for all the mutual abasement, the members of the family cannot quite extinguish the elementary need for love which is the more apparent the more they attempt to distort it. Lenny may be irredeemable but, in the final tableau, Joey's gesture of emotional submission to Ruth finds expression for a need beneath articulation. Even in a body of work distinguished by powerful closures, the final images of *The Homecoming* refuse to fade long after an actual production.

Pinter has always been concerned with the design of his plays, declaring in an interview with Lawrence Bensky, 'For me everything has to do with shape, structure and overall unity.'[5] The use of names and naming contributes to this. In *The Birthday Party* Act One opens with 'Is that you, Petey?' Act Two with the encounter of McCann and Stanley:

> McCann. My name's McCann.
> Stanley. Staying here long?
> McCann. Not long. What's your name?
> Stanley. Webber.

The opening of Act Three duplicates that of Act One, evoking an inconsequential everyday atmosphere with Petey sitting there reading his newspaper again, but this time Meg's question has a devastating variant, 'Is that you, Stan?' We have just witnessed the collapse of that identity and our expectations are the exact opposite of Meg's. She anticipates the familiar, we the fearful. A longer illustration shows how Pinter can use names and naming as part of the structural movement, here part of the emotional shaping at the close of Act

119

One, for overwhelming dramatic effect. 'Goldberg' is an innocuous Jewish surname, yet again we find the fearful in the familiar:

> STANLEY. (*coming down*). What are they called? What are their names?
> MEG. Oh, Stanley, I can't remember.
> STANLEY. They told you, didn't they? Or didn't they tell you?
> MEG. Yes, they . . .
> STANLEY. Then what are they? Come on. Try to remember.
> MEG. Why, Stan? Do you know them?
> STANLEY. How do I know if I know them until I know their names?
> MEG. Well . . . he told me, I remember.
> STANLEY. Well?
>
> *She thinks*
>
> MEG. Gold-something.
> STANLEY. Goldsomething?
> MEG. Yes, Gold . . .
> STANLEY. Yes?
> MEG. Goldberg.
> STANLEY. Goldberg?
> MEG. That's right. That was one of them.
>   STANLEY *slowly sits at table, left.*
>   Do you know them?
>   STANLEY *does not answer.*

Stanley's foreboding is heightened by the shock of the name.[6] His suppressed fears find vent in the frenzy which follows, the pounding on the drum closing the act. The movement from such indecisive, stunted dialogue to the action itself is also emotionally draining for the audience.

The structural circularity of *The Birthday Party* is even more explicit in *The Basement*. Here Pinter uses names with economy and simple force in that the closing lines are an exact inversion of those which open the play:

> LAW. (*With great pleasure*). Stott!
> STOTT. (*Smiling*). Hullo, Tim.
>
> STOTT. (*With great pleasure*). Law!
> LAW. (*Smiling*). Hullo, Charles.

Nothing could be simpler, yet the context leading to the last quote makes us recognize the subtexts of both. The affected use of the surname gives the formal a special kind of familiarity, which registers a mannered regard, simultaneously accommodating surprise and evoking a past guardedness. The *great pleasure* provides an appropriately exaggerated rhetorical gambit which the response complements with its defenceless, yet patronizing friendliness. The uniformity of masculine rivalry and aggression beneath individual identity are thus concisely indicated by the circularity, duplication and inter-changeability of the structural inversion.

The use of names as a kind of structural frame had also been anticipated by *A Night Out*. At the outset Mrs. Stokes repeatedly addresses her son using the proprietorial weight of his full christian name—'Albert' is the first word of the play and occurs six more times in the opening dialogue in tones of cumulative reproach. At the office party, after the incident for which Albert is blamed, Gidney shows all the intuition of a born tormentor. Having earlier rebuked 'Stokes', his office inferior, he intuitively adopts maternal tones to get at this 'mother's boy'.

> GIDNEY. I was telling you, Albert—
> ALBERT. Stokes.
> GIDNEY. I was telling you, Albert, that if you're going to behave like a boy of ten in mixed company—
> ALBERT. I told you my name is Stokes!
> GIDNEY. Don't be childish, Albert. (I. 229)

At the close, after his bullying triumph over the prostitute, Albert returns home to—'Albert!' (I. 231) which is repeated six times thereafter, exactly balancing the opening sequence. We have suspected Albert's violence towards his mother since it is included with the fantasies he engaged in with the prostitute. Thus that 'Albert!' has a confirmatory weight for us and him. The inescapability of his identity as 'mother's boy' is affirmed. This structural use of a name identifying a relation-ship is found, perhaps most pungently in all of Pinter's plays, in *Betrayal*.

The *a posteriori* structure of *Betrayal*, moving backwards in time, creates two primary expectations—how did the affair between Jerry and Emma start, and when and how did Robert learn of it? The latter occurs while Robert and Emma are holidaying in Venice. Robert realizes what is going on when Jerry's letter to Emma is brought to his attention in the American Express offices:

> . . . I mean, just because my name is Downs and your name is Downs doesn't mean that we're the Mr. and Mrs. Downs that they, in their laughing Mediterranean way, assume we are. We could be, and in fact are vastly more likely to be, total strangers. So let's say I, whom they laughingly assume to be your husband, had taken the letter, having declared myself to be your husband but in truth being a total stranger. . . . (IV. 218)

This is the first and only time in the play that their married names and titles are referred to. The irony is transparent but no less powerful for being so. As public expression of, at best, married love, the social identity of the shared married name has been rendered meaningless by betrayal, and Robert finds himself 'laughingly' a stranger. His continuing insinuation is painfully apparent and Emma feels forced to confirm Robert's intuition with 'We're lovers' (IV. 222).

As aspects of structure we find familiar names used towards the close of *Tea Party* and *The Homecoming*. That is, in both cases though the naming is limited to an instance, nevertheless it will be shown to reflect on the concerns of the play as a whole. In *Tea Party* Disson, at the stage of final collapse, is deaf to his mother's distraught cry 'Bobbie!' (III. 147). Disson has been 'Robert' to others throughout the play. The distance between the social milieux represented by the users of the names represents the social distance Disson has travelled and consequently the growing insecurity that brings him down. In contrast to the formal 'Robert' his brother-in-law has adopted the familiar upper-class version of his name, William. 'Willy' is the name by which he is introduced to Disson. Evidently this upper-class aspect of his new relations is part of Disson's insecurity. After drunkenly aspersing the beauties of Sunderley, the family seat, he takes the opportunity of getting at the public school resonances of 'Willy' by imposing his lower-class version—'Mind how you tread, Bill. Mind . . . how you tread, old Bill, old boy, old Bill' (III. 135). Again, in *The Homecoming*, a familiar form is used at a structurally crucial moment. As Teddy is about to leave, Ruth uses for the first and only time a personalized name deriving from the intimacy of their relationship—'Eddie' (III. 96). Teddy turns, there is a pause, and then the possible sense of appeal is quashed by the cliché of a whore's farewell, 'Don't become a stranger.' Ruth's words conflate the milieux of home and brothel reflecting her compound rôle of mother-lover-whore, an identity rather more complex than the earlier comic typecasting of tarts' typologies.

> LENNY. No, we'd call her something else. Dolores, or something.
> MAX. Or Spanish Jacky.
> LENNY. No, you've got to be reserved about it, Dad. We could call her something nice . . . like Cynthia . . . or Gillian.
>
> *Pause*
>
> JOEY. Gillian. (III. 90)

In *The Homecoming* Pinter recognized that Ruth's rôle actually fulfilled a psychological reality which subsumes social identity. In contrast earlier plays had more simply examined rôles in terms of pretence, delusion or, yet again, power struggles. 'Sally Gibbs' identifies the respectable teacher and student of foreign languages in *Night School*, but 'Katina' identifies the brash night-club hostess whose very coarseness reveals the day-time rôle to be a pretence. The prostitute of *A Night Out* still tries in the course of soliciting to pass herself off as a respectable middle-class mother, by confounding psychological defensiveness with rationalization—'All I do, I just entertain a few gentlemen, of my own choice, now and again. What girl doesn't?' (I. 241). In a more dramatically and sexually stylized context, Richard and Sarah, Windsor residents of stockbroker-belt respectability, take on initially exclusive rôles as lover, mistress and whore. 'Max', 'Dolores' and 'Mary' enact sexual fantasies that are part of a power-subservience relationship in fact determined by Sarah but eventually undermined and reversed by Richard (*The Lover*).

Clearly names and naming contribute to Pinter's aesthetic as a whole, but sometimes to a questionable extent—particularly in *No Man's Land*. When Foster first encounters

Spooner he seizes on his seeming unwillingness to introduce himself and uses names in a sardonic and threatening manner.

> His name's Friend. This is Mr. Briggs. Mr. Friend—Mr. Briggs. I'm Mr. Foster. Old English stock. John Foster. Jack. Jack Foster. Old English name. Foster. John Foster, Jack Foster. Foster. This man's name is Briggs. (IV. 98)

Such a verbal barrage pounds an introduction into a conclusion. That's as far as Spooner will get with them. Having more formally done so earlier to Hirst, Spooner eventually introduces himself (IV. 101). Thus in the first act the identity of Spooner is conspicuously established. The critical problem arises with the second act. Here, upon Hirst's elegant, sober and seemingly self-possessed entry, Spooner appears to have taken on a particular identity for him—'Charles. How nice of you to drop in.' (IV. 126). Then, after mutual revelations of scandalous past behaviour, Hirst retorts 'You are clearly a lout. The Charles Wetherby I knew was a gentleman' (IV. 136). The alternative naming initially gives rise to comic incredulity which could be discussed in relation to other moments of music-hall humour in the play, but *No Man's Land* is primarily realistic and on this level it is difficult to believe that the two elderly men who have spent some time drinking together have not recognized each other as former friends of university days. Particularly when Hirst has become famous and Spooner is the 'friend' he cuckolded with protracted deliberation. Pinter appears to make some uncomfortable concessions towards realism: 'I know that man' (IV. 114) says Hirst, and after being greeted as 'Charles' in the next act, Spooner says of Hirst 'I thought his face was familiar' (IV. 125). But surely improbability outweighs probability? It might be argued that Hirst's stupor and subsequent recognition of 'Charles Wetherby' in fact *symbolizes* his two worlds of drunkenness and sobriety, abandonment and control, the private man, the public author, night and day. Nevertheless, by 1975 Pinter's dramatic mode had become so established and familiar that instead of this kind of 'alienation effect' conditioning the audience's response it can possibly lead to the charge of mannerism. There is some irony here since the use

124

of another kind of 'alienation effect' in relation to names and naming successfully contributes to Pinter's unique accomplishments.

Brecht's concept of *verfremdung* or 'making strange', generally known as the 'alienation effect', characterized his mature theory and practice in the creation of an 'epic' theatre.[7] He believed that this kind of theatre must react against what he saw as the Aristotelian bourgeois theatre of empathy and mimetic illusion in which the audience was made to identify with the stage identity and situation of the characters through emotion. In contrast, Brecht both made innovations and also explored the resources of pre-naturalist theatre in order to ensure his audience's objectivity and criticism. The alienation effect, by way of such things as lighting, songs, placards and acting styles, was intended to prevent this false identification. Pinter has his own distinctive alienation effect created above all by laughter, but also by the dual mode of presences who remain unnamed and those absent who are made present by naming.

A considerable number of Pinter's characters are either unnamed in the play or unnamed under the *dramatis personae*: Mick and Aston (*The Caretaker*), Beth and Duff (*Landscape*), Ellen, Rumsey and Bates (*Silence*), Deeley (*Old Times*), Hirst (*No Man's Land*), Hornby (*A Kind of Alaska*), the speakers of *Dialogue for Three, Monologue, Family Voices* and *Victoria Station*. Here we have something of a paradox. Why is it that Pinter chooses to give some characters names when they remain unnamed in the course of the play? Presumably his initial conception of a character includes a name which acts as a kind of referential focus for the dramatist in writing, a focus which is withheld from the audience in performance (unless they have *read* the play, programme, cast list or review). The plays in which characters are completely unnamed either onstage or in the *dramatis personae*, are largely studies in isolation in which anonymity is an appropriate corollary. In both cases Pinter is depriving the audience of what is conventionally included as part of dramatic exposition—people quickly identified by names by which they are thus recognized, assimilated and known: an essential step in the process of dramatic empathy.

Pinter's kind of alienation effect denies the audience access to an identity by way of a name, a social procedure conventionally duplicated by drama. Instead we are exposed to existences, or rather what existences have become. This is Pinter's most remarkable existential quality, the rendering of just being, existing. And where the particular existence is anonymous an empathetic audience response is forestalled. The plays are powerful emotional experiences and the power partly derives from the alienation of emotion. We are always at a distance, separated from Pinter's characters, and vice versa. This is not to say that these characters, however concrete, thereby simply become symbolic cyphers merging into an abstract indeterminate place. Again names provide a focus on the real world, the names of places and pubs. For example, in *The Caretaker*, Davies and the unnamed Mick and Aston were often seen as allegorical and symbolic figures by early commentators. A German production dismayed Pinter when he saw that the director had replaced the attic ceiling with bare joists which revealed the sky above, implying some macro-microcosmic symbolic relationship. Yet in Mick's speeches and throughout the play the attic is set solidly in the actual world of London—of Balls Pond Road, Shepherds Bush, Acton, Wembley, Watford, and so on. Thus, with the filming of the play, Pinter was gratified that the realistic mode pre-empted any symbolism:

> . . . these characters move in the context of a real world . . . In the play, when people were confronted with just a set, a room and a door, they often assumed it was all taking place in limbo, in a vacuum, and the world outside hardly existed. . . .

And then, in praising the director's visual focus on the characters themselves in the extramural scenes, Pinter added, crucially, '. . . and while we go into the world outside it is almost as if only these characters exist.'[8] This takes us to the heart of Pinter's writing. The world is real enough, the characters are solid, concrete, and yet there is a kind of dislocation between the two. In plays like *Old Times* and *No Man's Land* the objective world of London is solidly evoked in terms of places and pubs—'The Wayfarers Tavern, just off the Brompton Road' (IV. 44), 'The Bull's Head in Chalk Farm' (IV. 99)—yet the characters seem to exist tangentially in relation to it.

Generally speaking, after the first unfocused locale of *The*

Room, Pinter chose to counter and qualify any movement towards the symbolic or abstract by specific topographical reference. In the most recent work, *Other Places,* however comically contrasted the isolated night voices of the controller and driver of *Victoria Station,* the solidity of the station and Crystal Palace provide a local habitation and a name. The naïvely epicene young speaker of *Family Voices,* seemingly immured in the bizarre *menage* of the Witherses, gives some credibility to his relation in the all too mundane reference to 'The Fishmonger's Arms' in 'this enormous city' (p. 68). *A Kind of Alaska* is the remote frozen waste of an adult life exiled in the coma of sleeping sickness, a life which awakes to the past and present of Hastings and Torquay, Fulham and Townley Street. In these juxtapositions of large actual world and specific individuals, Pinter contrasts the permanent and impermanent, the fixed and the temporary, the peripheries of place and what I term the tangency of being.

This concept, the tangency of being, will be clarified in consideration of the final category of naming. The following is a selective list of those, either from the past or in the present, who are given a kind of presence in the act of naming: Uncle Barney and Eddie (*The Birthday Party*), George 'Whatsisname' ('Last to Go'), Cavendish (*A Slight Ache*), MacGregor and Jessie (*The Homecoming*), Hawkins (*The Collection*), Doughty ('Night'), Mr. Sykes (*Landscape*), McCabe *et al* (*Old Times*), Boris, Hugo, the Winstanleys *et al* (*No Man's Land*), Casey and Spinks (*Betrayal*), the Witherses (*Family Voices*). Uncle Barney is only known to Goldberg who, in turn, does not know Lulu's Eddie. Cavendish is known to Edward but not to the match-seller, Hawkins to James but not to Bill, and so on. In this Pinter implies that human existence is largely alienated, each person consisting of a series of past tangencies, both touching on and glancing off such another in the present. Perhaps the best example of this, incorporating the function of naming, is the exchange at the beginning of the party, between McCann and Meg—'Ever been to Carrikmacross?' 'I've been to King's Cross' (I. 69). In writing Pinter always has the picture-frame stage in mind.[9] This creates a physical tangent dividing audience and actors which contributes to the alienation effect of emotional distancing. Then again this kind of estranged

127

relationship is internalized in the play itself by the above-named 'presences' who remain at one remove from the audience and often from some of the characters onstage to whom the person named is unknown, as we have seen.

Pinter's writing implicitly rejects the humanist assumption of dramatic art as a mode which expresses and affirms the duplication of shared experience seeing the stage and what takes place on it as a microcosm of the audience's world. Pinter exploits names and naming for dramatic alienation as an expressive form for the social alienation of this tangency of being and exposure of existences. The residual experience of Pinter's plays is of a fundamental awareness that to exist is to exist alone; as Goldberg puts it, 'We all wander on our tod through this world. It's a lonely pillow to kip on' (II. 66). It is in this that Pinter is an existentialist writer, but of a particular kind.

It is not uncommon to find Pinter described as an existential writer and Walter Kerr in fact devoted his 1967 study to the approach.[10] Kerr examines the plays in general terms deriving from Sartre's philosophy of man as unformed, open and free to act in the void in which he finds himself. Character is a potency, a possibility, fluid and mobile. Kerr focuses on Ruth in *The Homecoming*, and here he does have a point but elsewhere almost all of his judgements are misplaced. Apart from Ruth, Pinter's characters appear to live an 'inauthentic' existence in 'bad faith', i.e. the negative rather than the positive aspect of Sartre's existentialism. Above all, the characters are defined by the limiting nature of existence itself which is not just the fact of external circumstance but comes from within their own inner limitation. They all manifest a fixity, what existences have become, the particular fashioning of time and habit.[11] Here there is simply no possibility of the central transcendence of existentialism: that in full recognition of his own nothingness in a world bereft of absolute value, man can find a principle of being and action—Heidegger's 'authentic' life. In eschewing exposition and generally following limited continuous time spans, Pinter's plays present an existential continuum in which, most forcefully where the characters are either unnamed or nameless, identity is co-extensive with being. Within this continuum whoever or whatever a person is, or may be, is identified by the nature of their language: 'a language that speaks us instead of a language that is spoken by us'.[12] Pinter has referred to speech as 'a constant stratagem to cover nakedness' (I. 15). However, this stratagem often has the reverse effect on an audience. In the attempt to conceal the character is revealing his being in the exposure of language itself. What has shaped the life has shaped the language.

Perhaps this is why Pinter insisted on the script changes for *Betrayal* in which the name would indicate a speaker rather than an identity and the increased spacing emphasized separation rather than communication. Inevitably it must be asked 'What's in a name?'—evidently, for Harold Pinter, so much.

NOTES

1. The *Guardian*, Tuesday 13 June 1978. In the course of this essay the following plays are discussed or referred to (dates of composition are given, see Steven H. Gale, *Harold Pinter An Annotated Bibliography*, Boston, 1978): *The Room, The Birthday Party, The Dumb Waiter*, 1957; *A Slight Ache*, 1958; *The Caretaker, A Night Out*, 'Last to Go', 'Dialogue for Three', 1959; *Night School, The Dwarfs*, 1960; *The Collection*, 1961; *The Lover*, 1962; *The Basement*, 1963; *Tea Party, The Homecoming*, 1964; *Landscape*, 1967; *Silence*, 1968; 'Night', 1969; *Old Times*, 1970; *Monologue*, 1972; *No Man's Land*, 1974; *Betrayal*, 1978. These works are collected in *Plays: One, Plays: Two, Plays: Three, Plays: Four* (London, Eyre Methuen, respectively 1976, 1977, 1978, 1981), to which reference will be made quoting volume and page number. References to *The Hothouse* and *Other Places* are to the Eyre Methuen editions of 1980 and 1982.
2. *The Dumb Waiter* and *The Dwarfs* are the only exceptions in Pinter's work.
3. Katherine H. Burkman, inspired by Frazer's *The Golden Bough*, considers Flora as fertility goddess naming the matchseller after the saint's day which coincides with the summer solstice, and Edward as the dying god (*The Dramatic World of Harold Pinter: Its Basis in Ritual*, Columbus, 1971).
4. For some further examples see pp. 80–1, 84–5.
5. In Arthur Ganz (ed.), *Pinter: A Collection of Critical Essays* (Englewood Cliffs, 1972), p. 33.
6. This is a specific aspect of Pinter's poem 'A View of the Party' (*Poems*, London, 1968, p. 17.)

> The thought that Goldberg was
> A man to dread and know
> Jarred Stanley in the blood
> When, still, he heard his name.

7. See John Willett (ed.), *Brecht on Theatre* (London, 1964). Victor E. Amend finds a 'kinship' with Brecht in Pinter's alienation effect of emotional distancing which he considers a limitation ('Harold Pinter: Some Credits and Debits' *Modern Drama*, 10, No. 2, 1967, 165–67).

8. 'Filming "The Caretaker" ', *Transatlantic Review*, 13, 1963, 23.

9. 'Whenever I write for the stage I merely see the stage I've been used to. . . . I always think of the normal picture-frame stage which I used as an actor'—'Introduction. Writing for Myself' (II. 9).

10. *Harold Pinter* (New York, 1967).

11. 'I'm afraid society is a pattern which does kill and crab and confine, and that at the same time the individuals who make the society do the same for themselves by conforming to their own habits continually day after day and year after year'—*The Rising Generation. No. 7—A Playwright—Harold Pinter*, an interview with John Sherwood, B.B.C. European Service, 3 March 1960, B.B.C. Transcript p. 6.

12. I adapt the telling sentence of Guido Almansi and Simon Henderson from their *Harold Pinter* (London, 1983), p. 41.

7

Death and the Double in Three Plays by Harold Pinter

by KATHERINE H. BURKMAN

> And what's a double? Well, in Scotland, when I was a boy, we
> had a name for such things. If a man met a creature like himself
> in the lane, or in town, maybe in the dark, 'twas a sure sign of ill
> luck or even death.[1]

Confrontation with death provides the ultimate test in Harold
Pinter's dramatic world of one's ability to live a meaningful
life. Pinter's characters meet that test in a variety of ways in
his different plays, so that we have everything from the
victimized Stanley of *The Birthday Party*, sacrificed by represen-
tatives of the system he would flee, to the more rebellious Ruth
of *The Homecoming*, sacrificing her American life and identity—
the death need not be literal—in order to return to her
English identity and embrace a new life with her husband's
family. In three of Pinter's major plays, *A Slight Ache* (1961),
Old Times (1971) and *No Man's Land* (1975), confrontation with
death involves the struggle of the protagonist with a double. In
these dramas, the protagonists' encounters with a double
initiate an inward journey which brings them face to face both
with their mortality and with previously unknown aspects of
themselves.

Pinter's doubles in the plays under consideration, the

131

matchseller who stands at the back gate of Edward's house in *A Slight Ache*, Anna, Kate's room-mate of twenty years ago, who has come to visit her in *Old Times*, and Spooner, the elderly tramp whom the writer Hirst has met at a pub and brought home for a drink in *No Man's Land*, elude the neat classification that some doubles have achieved in literary tradition. They are not what Robert Rogers has called manifest doubles, recognizable by the characters they resemble or other characters in the play as the protagonists' physical doubles,[2] nor are they mere figments of the protagonists' imaginations, hallucinatory projections of characters who cast forth repressed parts of their own divided selves. The doubles also fail to perform as allegorical figures, guardian angels or devils, the better or evil part of the soul come to save or damn the protagonists whose doubles they are. Yet these Pinter doubles are partially the central characters' mirror images, partially their projections, and partially allegorical figures of good and evil come to save or damn them.[3]

In *A Slight Ache*, the matchseller, a tramp who stinks, wears old clothes, and is blind in at least one eye, would seem to bear no physical resemblance to Edward, a country gentleman who writes philosophical essays. Yet when Edward invites the tramp inside in order to expose him as an imposter, we realize, as Edward's physical strength wanes, that we have two old men before us. If Edward does not resemble the matchseller at the onset of the play, he soon becomes the 'great bullockfat of jelly'[4] that he tells his wife Flora the matchseller is. The matchseller, who looks very different to Edward at different times and appears to be laughing at him one minute, crying for him the next, becomes, in Edward's eyes, a kind of mirror image whose shifting reflections reveal Edward to himself.

Contrasting physical types in *Old Times* also come to seem very much alike or even identical. Kate initially remembers her ex-room-mate as 'fuller' than she, and their contrasting dispositions suggest contrasting physical types. Anna is vivacious, outgoing, restless and flirtatious, while Kate is domestic, shy, solitary and a dreamer. Kate's husband Deeley, however, remembers the two now middle-aged women in ways that suggest that they were so alike as to be the same person. He first recalls looking up their skirts at a party; and then, using information Kate has given him about Anna stealing her underwear, he suggests that Anna not only wore Kate's underwear, she also pretended to be Kate:

> On the way to the party I took her into a café, bought her a cup of coffee, beards with faces. She thought she was you, said little, so little. Maybe she was you. Maybe it was you, having coffee with me, saying little, so little.[5]

As with Edward and the matchseller, initially opposing physical types seem, on one level, to become identical.

Hirst and Spooner in *No Man's Land* again appear as opposing physical types, Spooner a failed, shabbily dressed poet, Hirst a successful, 'precisely' attired writer. We see them on stage, however, both elderly and increasingly inebriated; and Spooner emphasizes his kinship with Hirst to Foster and Briggs, Hirst's servants. 'He has grandchildren. As have I. As I have. We both have fathered. We are of an age. I know his wants. . . .'[6] At the end of the first act, Hirst begins to feel he knows Spooner, 'I know that man' (p. 114), and Spooner identifies himself as the man drowning in Hirst's dream; in Act II Hirst identifies Spooner as his old friend and sexual rival, Charles Wetherby. As in *Old Times* memory defeats differences, conjuring up that physical and psychological identity that we may not actually see but which nevertheless is strongly suggested.

The term *Doppelganger*, which literally means 'double-goer' originated with the novelist Jean Paul Richter in 1796 and referred to 'people who see themselves'.[7] Subsequently the word *Doppelganger* and its English translation, double, came to refer to the one seen, the character who resembles the protagonist and is encountered by him rather than the protagonist himself. From a psychological viewpoint, even though the character seen by the protagonist may be referred to as the double, the doubling process, as Robert Rogers has pointed out, often involves decomposition of a whole character,[8] so that one may think of each character as a double of the other or part of a whole. By providing amorphous doubles whom the protagonists only gradually come to see as themselves, Pinter offers three dramas in which the latent becomes manifest and coming to see oneself in another involves a growth in self-knowledge. As they come to recognize themselves in their doubles, Pinter's protagonists come to understand themselves as double or partial human beings.

The possibility that Pinter's three doubles are mere projections of the protagonists, which would make the dramas totally intra-psychic, is undermined, however, because the doubles interact with other characters, even appearing in scenes in which the protagonists for whom they are doubles are absent. The matchseller interacts with Edward's wife Flora, Anna with Kate's husband Deeley, and Spooner with Hirst's servants Foster and Briggs. Yet Flora and Edward describe the matchseller in such opposite ways (Edward sees him as 'jelly', Flora as 'solid') that one can understand Martin Esslin's contention that the old tramp is their shared projection.[9] And since Anna is present when Kate and Deeley discuss her imminent arrival, merely turning into the action from her position on stage, one gets the impression that she is a latent part of Kate, part of her past that has lingered on and re-emerges. Deeley's assertion that Anna, whom he claims to have known in the past, used to pretend to be Kate and might even have been her, offers one the possibility that just as Flora and Edward may have projected the matchseller, so Deeley and Kate may have projected Anna. Because Spooner, like the matchseller and Anna, is perceived in amorphous fashion to reflect whatever the protagonist perceives at a particular moment, a stranger taken home for a drink, an old friend and rival, he too may be regarded partially as a projection of Hirst's unconscious desires and fears.

That the three Pinter doubles are more than other characters' projections is not simply due to their partially independent actions with other characters, for one could argue that they are group projections and hence are free to operate without the protagonists' presence. Their stature as independent characters comes, rather, from the allegorical component of their rôles. Just as Pinter's latent doubles become manifest only by the end of each play, and just as they operate partially as independent characters and partially as projections of the protagonists, so too they lack allegorical status but have enough mythic dimension and symbolic significance to become borderline allegorical figures as well. At this allegorical level, Pinter transcends psychology, and characters who might have become case histories gain archetypal resonance. At this level too, the protagonists' encounters with their doubles become confrontations with death, confrontations that involve the ultimate question of their salvation or damnation.

From the outset, *A Slight Ache*'s matchseller is a figure of mystery. Flora believes he arrives at the house each morning because he is there when she awakens, but Edward reminds her that she never sees him arrive, the implication being that he is always there. The matchseller's silence adds to the mysterious, inhuman nature of that presence. Flora and Edward's contrasting visions of him that unite only in seeing him as a bullock may lead one to associate him with the god Dionysus who was often known to take the form of a bull. The matchseller, it would appear then, is not so much unreal in nature as surreal or even supernatural.

As Edward falters before the mysterious presence, we soon realize, as he does, that he is dying. Projecting his own physical discomfort onto the matchseller, 'What is it, damn you. You're shivering. You're sagging' (p. 27), he identifies with his antagonist's supposed weakness, 'Aaah! You've sat at last. What a relief. You must be tired . . .' (p. 27), but then finds himself having difficulty breathing: 'I must get some air. I must get a breath of air' (p. 27). When Flora suggests that the matchseller is dying, Edward, who has come to identify himself with the old man, protests vehemently but finally succumbs to his own death. As Edward falls to the ground, clearly defeated, the matchseller rises and is taken over by Flora, who gives her dying husband the matchseller's box.

The rôle of the double as death has been discussed by Otto Rank, who suggests that initially doubles represented eternal life and only subsequently came to symbolize death or came to stand for death itself.[10] The matchseller, however, operates both as a herald of death or death's personification and as a herald of new life. His association with death has largely to do with his silence, which operates as a weapon that turns Edward continually back upon himself and forces him to use the matchseller as a mirror in which he may come to see his dying self. Freud, who found dumbness or silence to represent death in dreams, myths and fairy tales, suggests that characters in literature who are silent often represent the Goddess of Death.[11] Hence, for example, by rejecting the silent Cordelia, Lear avoids only for a time that inevitable embracing of death which is his and all men's fate.[12] So, too, when Edward invites the silent matchseller into his home does he begin that encounter with death that in his case involves an encounter with self and the emergence of a new self.

In his rôle as Death, then, the matchseller provides Edward with the opportunity to confront his own mortality. And though Edward seems defeated by the confrontation, that defeat has overtones of tragic dimension that involve the victory of self-knowledge. In coming to see himself more clearly in his double, Edward comes to see not so much what he is but what he is not and has not been; the series of clichés with which he describes his life come to seem both pathetic and ridiculous to him, and he imagines the matchseller laughing at him and crying for him (p. 37). Like Oedipus, who blinds himself when he achieves insight, Edward's diminishing sight, the slight ache in his eyes, seems to take place as he suffers new insight into himself and his situation.

But since the matchseller seems, on another level, to be a part of Edward that rises as he falls, not a mere projection, but an ongoing, younger, stronger self, Edward's defeat has overtones of comic dimension as well that involve the victory of rebirth. Falling to the floor near the end of the play, Edward continues to address the matchseller:

> Not that I had any difficulty in seeing you, no, no, it was not so much my sight, my sight is excellent—in winter I run about with nothing on but a pair of polo shorts—no, it was not so much any deficiency in my sight as the airs between me and my object—don't weep—the change of air, the currents obtaining in the space between me and my object, the shades they make, the shapes they take, the quivering, the eternal quivering—please stop crying—nothing to do with heat-haze. Sometimes, of course, I would take shelter, shelter to compose myself. Yes, I would seek a tree, a cranny of bushes, erect my canopy and so make shelter. And rest. (*Low murmur.*) And then I no longer heard the wind or saw the sun. Nothing entered, nothing left my nook. I lay on my side in my polo shorts, my fingers lightly in contact with the blades of grass, the earthflowers, the petals

of the earthflowers flaking, lying on my palm, the underside of all the great foliage dark, above me, but it is only afterwards I say the foliage was dark, the petals flaking, then I said nothing, I remarked nothing, things happened upon me, then in my times of shelter, the shades, the petals, carried themselves, carried their bodies upon me, and nothing entered my nook, nothing left it.

(*Pause*)

But then, the time came. I saw the wind. I saw the wind, swirling, and the dust at my back gate, lifting, and the long grass, scything together . . . (*Slowly, in horror.*) You are laughing. You're laughing. Your face. Your body. (*Overwhelming nausea and horror.*) Rocking . . . gasping . . . rocking . . . shaking . . . rocking . . . heaving . . . rocking . . . You're laughing at me! Aaaaahhhh!

The MATCHSELLER *rises. Silence.*

You look younger. You look extraordinarily . . . youthful. (pp. 38–9)

As Edward seems almost to give birth to a new self, in Frazerian terms he is the god of winter giving way to the god of summer, a dying and reviving god.[13] Having shown himself ignorant of Flora and the garden over which she presides, having referred to the beautiful summer day as 'treacherous', and having combated the 'first wasp of summer' as if it were a deadly enemy, Edward's wintry identity gives way to his summer self (Flora has associated the matchseller with sexuality and has recognized him as the incarnation of summer when naming him Barnabus, which means summer).[14] On this ritual level of the play's action, Edward plays the part of himself and his double; he is the dying god who rises anew, and Flora is the tragicomic fertility goddess, the unfaithful/ faithful wife, who presides over the ritual death and renewal.

As the embodiment of Edward's repressed self, the matchseller is something of what Keppler designates as a 'vision of horror' whose advent suggests the threat of death not through anything he does but through his mere presence.[15] As the allegorical embodiment of summer, however, the matchseller suggests the new life that must emerge as the wintry Edward dies. Representing the height of summer, the matchseller is also dying; Flora says she will buy him 'toys to play with' on his deathbed (p. 33), but the youthful guise Edward sees him in stands for that part of summer which at play's end Flora suggests is just arriving.

The matchseller as a 'vision of horror' double is replaced in Pinter's later play, *Old Times*, by what Keppler refers to as a tempter double.[16] But Anna, a past self who makes her claim on Kate in this play, is not victorious; unlike Edward, Kate does not submit and it is the double, Anna, who must die. The doubling issue is somewhat different here, too, in that Anna serves as a double for both Kate and her husband Deeley, whom in some ways she resembles more than she resembles Kate. The results of her exorcism by Kate, then, affect Kate's marriage which lies in ruins at the play's end.

Anna's quasi-allegorical rôle as a temptress who seeks Kate's damnation is suggested by her attempt to possess Kate. Luring Kate back twenty years through memory to a time in which they shared an apartment and a life together in London, Anna excludes Deeley in order to reassert her claims. When Anna rattles off a list of memories about their life as 'innocent girls, innocent secretaries', with 'the sheer expectation of it all', Deeley resists—'We rarely get to London'—while Kate shows interest—'Yes, I remember' (p. 18). Anna's memories of a man 'crying in our room' (p. 32), whom she rejects and who disappears from Kate's life, are weapons that she uses successfully against Deeley, who re-enacts the memory of his being rejected at the end of the drama, becoming the 'odd man out' of the film each has claimed to see with Kate.

Although Kate is only temporarily ensnared by Anna, she seems at one point to be transported back to their earlier life, and behaves as if she is back there, discussing possible company to have over and clothes to wear. When Kate turns down Anna's offer to run her bath 'tonight' it is as if other nights that would be fine.

Kate's general remoteness from both Anna and Deeley, however, causes them to join forces against her and brings out their basic similarity. Unlike Kate, who is self-contained and content with her country life, Anna and Deeley are restless, 'volcanic' types; Deeley claims to know the volcanic island that Anna describes as her home: 'I've been there' (p. 22), he asserts. One can see, too, that Deeley's possessiveness proves as threatening to Kate as does that of her former roommate. 'And someday I'll know that moment divine,/ When all the things you are, are mine!' (p. 27) Deeley sings in counterpoint to Anna's memories of song fragments, excluding Kate who later objects to being talked about by both of them as if she were dead (p. 34).

The threat of death, then, comes from this darker, restless, repressed side of Kate with Anna producing that uncanny effect that Freud attributes to the emergence of the repressed.[17] What we have here, too, is a confrontation between a protagonist and her double that Keppler claims is rare, in which parts of the self from different times of development have 'mutual impact'[18] on one another. Kate is threatened, too, however, by her husband, who is attracted now to one side of her, now to another, but is essentially hostile to both.

Kate has described Anna to Deeley as a thief who stole her underwear; toward the end of the play Kate accuses Anna of trying to steal her smile as well and, by implication, her very self. When she calls upon memory to destroy Anna, 'But I remember you. I remember you dead' (p. 71), she goes on to describe Anna's failure to become her:

> You tried to do my little trick, one of my tricks you had borrowed, my little slow smile, my little slow shy smile, my bend of the head, my half closing of the eyes, that we knew so well, but it didn't work, the grin only split the dirt at the sides of your mouth and stuck. You stuck in your grin. (p. 72)

The exorcism of Anna is completed as Kate describes the 'lengthy bath' she then took and Deeley's arrival in the same room. It is only, however, after Kate rejects Deeley, whom she recalls did not permit her to plaster his face with dirt, that she tells him that no one had slept in the bed before him. Deeley had suggested a wedding and change of environment rather than the dirtying of his face, but Kate claims 'Neither mattered' (p. 73). Deeley is not able to accept that death and rebirth that Kate offers. Anna, however, is buried in dirt, and Kate, her other part, re-emerges with new life.

Through this symbolic annihilation of her double, Kate does not, it seems to me, as Lucina Gabbard suggests, rid herself of a repressed 'earthy, sensual self'.[19] On the contrary, she rids herself of a possessive, homosexual self (Anna's and Kate's relationship has taken on lesbian tones, suggested by Anna's exploits in Kate's underwear which she tells Deeley she shared with her room-mate in the dark, pp. 55–6) who is actually very like her husband for whom, as I previously suggested, Anna is also a double.[20] What Kate actually overcomes, then, is a narcissistic self-love which leaves her free not only of a more infantile self but of an infantile husband who is not able to participate in Kate's rebirth.[21]

Deeley's refusal of that death which promises rebirth aligns him with Hirst in *No Man's Land*, who similarly turns his back on that life-giving confrontation with death that Edward, by succumbing to his double, and Kate by defeating hers, achieve. Spooner offers himself to Hirst as a saviour who will oversee his literary comeback—'The young, I can assure you, would flock to hear you' (p. 90)—and a kind of sexual renewal through that comeback as well. Personifying the 'evening' as a woman, Spooner says: 'Let us content ourselves with the idea of an intimate reading, in a pleasing and conducive environment, let us consider an evening to be remembered, by all who take part in her' (p. 91). Hirst's rejection of Spooner—'Let us change the subject' (p. 91), he says—allows Foster, one of his servant/henchmen, to designate that changed subject as an eternal winter in which he and Briggs, Hirst's other servant/henchman, will keep Hirst company.

Hirst finds in Spooner the same kind of threat of death that Edward found in the matchseller. Spooner has confronted him with his impotence, 'So you won't, I hope, object if I take out my prayer beads and my prayer mat and salute what I take to be your impotence' (p. 33), alternately playing the rôle of his rival and his friend. As a rival he questions Hirst's masculinity and poetic prowess—'I begin to wonder whether truly accurate and therefore essentially poetic definition means anything to you at all' (p. 31)—and as a friend, he offers himself as a servant, a caretaker, and above all as a means through death to renewal:

140

You need a friend. You have a long hike, my lad, up which, presently you slog unfriended. Let me perhaps be your boatman. For if and when we talk of a river we talk of a deep and dark architecture. (p. 33)

Spooner will go beyond ushering Hirst to death as a Charon; he will die for him—'I will accept death's challenge on your behalf' (p. 89). He even suggests that he has died for him. Hirst is bothered by a dream of someone drowning, a dream he returns to several times in the play, and when Spooner announces 'It was I drowning in your dream' (p. 47), Hirst falls to the floor. Shortly thereafter Hirst says 'I know that man' (p. 52), and one realizes that he is beginning to recognize the dying, impotent self that Spooner has accused him of being in Spooner, who is his double, and hence in himself.

The double behaviour of the doubles in each of these Pinter plays in which they are enemy/rivals of the protagonists one minute, friends the next, may be explained if one sees how for Pinter death is both an enemy and a friend. Confrontation with the double is in each case a confrontation with an enemy in so far as that double threatens death; the matchseller through silence, Anna through talking of Kate as if she were dead, and Spooner by casting aspersions on Hirst's masculinity and creativity. To some extent, too, each double embodies death: the matchseller as old and stinking presents Edward with an image of his own decay, Kate remembers Anna as dead, and Spooner presents himself as the drowned person in Hirst's dream.

By threatening death, however, each of Pinter's doubles offers the possibility of new life. The matchseller is more than Edward's friend; he is that other self, 'My nearest and dearest. My kith and kin' (p. 36), whom Edward's dying self gives birth to: 'You look younger. You look extraordinarily youthful' (p. 39). Because he is Edward's double, his other self, his winning of Flora's hand is not so much a defeat for Edward as a way in which death itself is conquered and Edward can live anew.

The threat of death to Kate is more severe as the neutral, passive matchseller is replaced by the possessive and destructive Anna. Because Anna is again Kate's double, her annihilation by Kate involves the death of a part of Kate, but in this case, too, death is liberating. Kate describes her cleansing bath after the event and her denial to Deeley of Anna's existence: 'He asked me once, at about that time, who had slept in that bed before him. I told him no one. No one at all' (p. 73). The Kate who emerges is stronger, less ambivalent, and free.

Hirst's failure to meet death's challenge may be due to the nature of his double, Spooner, whose rôle as saviour is even more spurious than that of the matchseller. He describes himself as a 'betwixt twig peeper' (p. 18) rather than a participator in life and suggests that he gets his strength from not having been loved. Despite his inadequacies, however, Spooner has had a vision of a fisher-king restored to fertility that he shares with Foster and Briggs. He describes a scene in a café in Amsterdam in which a fisherman lifted his catch high and was cheered by all present, a scene of joyous renewal observed by a whistling figure in the shadows. Spooner's admission that he has never painted the picture of that scene that he had hoped to paint leaves us with the impression that he has remained, as the figure in shadow, a mere shadow of what Hirst might become, but unlike Hirst he is still making an effort to realize his vision of renewal. When Briggs questions his rôle as a poet, suggesting that poets are young, Spooner replies 'I am young' (p. 64).

In Hirst's case, whatever inner potentiality is offered by Spooner is reduced partly by those other parts of Hirst, Foster and Briggs, who denigrate Spooner's offers of friendship to Hirst by reducing him to 'Mr. Friend' (p. 36). If these doubting doubles of Hirst act as defences against Spooner as a death/life force, Hirst's fear of his own death/rebirth may be clearly seen in his attitude toward his recurring dream and his final denial of the drowning that was the dream's centre. Hirst prefers and elects that death-in-life that Eliot portrays in *The Waste Land*, a no-man's land in which there can be no real death and hence no real life.

Pinter writes more fully, possibly, than any other modern playwright about the renewal of that death-in-life wasteland, a renewal that in all of his plays involves death. In *A Slight Ache*,

Old Times and *No Man's Land*, the protagonists' confrontations with death in a double are what initiate their journeys toward knowledge of the self. Edward's increasing knowledge in *A Slight Ache* clearly leads him to the death of his old self, and we see his new self emerge. Here the emphasis is on seasonal as well as personal renewal, and though the rhythms of death and rebirth may be cast in tragicomic and absurd tones, those rhythms nevertheless persist. In *Old Times*, we see an old self asserting claims that are defeated and the resulting destruction of a marriage, but here the self that rises anew appears to be more whole in her liberation—though possibly more lonely. In *No Man's Land*, despite Hirst's non-arrival at that knowledge of self that Edward and Kate achieve, the journey is illuminating. Though he retreats to a Beckettian landscape that is haunted with echoes of Eliot, a no-man's land situated between life and death, Hirst's flirtation with his spurious saviour/ double and his rejection of that death which might bring him new life provides us with insight into the dynamics of modern man's struggle with life and his retreat from living it fully.

In each case, the amorphous nature of Pinter's doubles is the source of the play's dynamics. By portraying the doubles as characters who are independent of the protagonists yet a part of them and as mysterious outer forces as well, Pinter offers a vision of life that has both psychological and spiritual dimension. Arising in part as narcissistic defences against death, the doubles continue to threaten death or stand for death itself.[22] In their dramatic encounters with death as a double, Pinter's characters must confront and accept their mortality if they are to arrive at any meaningful kind of existence. In *No Man's Land* the renewal of the English language itself is at stake. Paradoxically, it is death alone, for Pinter, that can offer any satisfaction to man's immortal longings, for without death there is no possibility of rebirth or renewal.

NOTES

1. Robertson Davies, *World of Wonders* (New York: Penguin Books, 1977), p. 188.
2. Robert Rogers, *A Psychoanalytical Study of the Double in Literature* (Detroit: Wayne State University Press, 1970), pp. 18–39.
3. C. F. Keppler, in *The Literature of the Second Self* (Tuscan: University of Arizona Press, 1972), prefers the kind of double that Pinter portrays and actually reserves the definition of the double as a second self for those double figures who are both objective and subjective in nature. 'He is always "there", a self in his own right, never translatable into a product of mental aberration; yet he is always "here" as well, his psyche intergrown by untraceable shared tendrils with that of his counterpart, and so never translatable into a purely external fellow being' (p. 10).
4. Harold Pinter, *A Slight Ache* in *Three Plays: A Slight Ache, The Collection, The Dwarfs* (New York: Grove Press, 1962), p. 29. All subsequent references to the play are from this edition and are hereafter given parenthetically in the body of the text.
5. Harold Pinter, *Old Times* (New York: Grove Press, 1971), p. 69. All subsequent references to the play are from this edition and are hereafter given parenthetically in the body of the text.
6. Harold Pinter, *No Man's Land* (New York: Grove Press, 1975), p. 47. All subsequent references to the play are from this edition and are hereafter given parenthetically in the body of the text.
7. Clifford Hallam, 'The Double as Incomplete Self: Toward a Definition of Doppelgänger', *Fearful Symmetry: Doubles and Doubling in Literature and Film* (Tallahassee: University Presses of Florida, 1981), p. 25.
8. Rogers, p. 4.
9. Martin Esslin, *The Theatre of the Absurd* (New York: Doubleday & Co., Anchor Books, 1961), p. 242.
10. Otto Rank, 'The Double as Immortal Self', *Beyond Psychology* (New York: Dover Publications, Inc., 1958), p. 76.
11. Sigmund Freud, 'The Theme of the Three Caskets', *The Standard Edition of the Complete Psychological Works of Sigmund Freud*, 24 vols., trans. and ed. by James Strachey (London: The Hogarth Press, 1938), 12:301.
12. Freud, p. 301.
13. Sir James Frazer, *The Golden Bough*, abr. edn. in one vol. (New York: Macmillan Co., 1951), pp. 377–456.
14. The day of Saint Barnabas, June eleventh in the old style calendar, was the day of the summer solstice, and Barnaby-bright is the name for the longest day and the shortest night of the year.
15. Keppler, p. 78.
16. Keppler, pp. 377–456.
17. Sigmund Freud, 'The "Uncanny" ', *The Standard Edition of the Complete Psychological Works of Sigmund Freud*, 24 vols., trans. and ed. by James Strachey (London: Hogarth Press, 1938), 17:176.
18. Keppler, p. 176.

19. Lucina Paquet Gabbard, *The Dream Structure of Pinter's Plays: A Psycho-analytic Approach* (Teaneck: Fairleigh Dickinson University Press, 1976), p. 250.
20. Judith A. Roof in her M.A. Thesis, 'Triangles and Doubles in Three Plays by Eugene O'Neill' (Columbus: Ohio State University, 1980), has examined a series of triangles in three plays by Eugene O'Neill in which such double doubling is the key to the dynamics of the triangle.
21. Although critics have tended to identify Kate as narcissistic, Anna as outgoing and sensuous, I think the narcissism is more centred in Anna. Kate is giving; she likes domesticity and has offered the dirt to each character that is part of her self in her rôle as Earth Mother. Anna is part of an earlier narcissistic stage that is making its claim but which Kate overcomes.
22. Otto Rank, *The Double: A Psychoanalytic Study*, trans. and ed. by Harry Tucker, Jr. (Chapel Hill: University of North Carolina Press, 1971), p. 71. Rank explains that while doubling grows out of a narcissistic inability to love others, and a fear of death, resisting exclusive self-love is what leads to the doubling and a projection of hate or fear onto the other self (p. 73). 'On the other hand, in the same phenomena of defense the threat also recurs, against which the individual wants to protect and assert himself' (p. 86).

8

Harold Pinter's *Family Voices* and the Concept of Family

by STEVEN H. GALE

Harold Pinter exhibits an ambivalent attitude toward the concept of family, off-stage and on. Early in 1975 I wrote to the playwright to see if he would be interested in a visiting professor's position. He wrote back saying that he was too involved with his family to leave London—that he would not even travel to New York to direct a play until after his son Daniel graduated from school. Less than four months later news of his affair with Lady Antonia Fraser was being reported in newspapers worldwide.

Pinter's plays exhibit the same ambiguity regarding the concept of family that the dramatist has displayed in his personal life. Although most of the scholarly consideration given to the subject as it appears in his dramaturgy has focused on *The Homecoming* (1965), the theme of family has been a central one in Pinter's work since his first play, *The Room* (1957), when Rose solicitously 'mothered' her husband, Bert. *The Birthday Party* (1958), *A Slight Ache* (1959), *The Caretaker* (1960), *Night School* (1960), *A Night Out* (1961), *The Collection* (1961), *The Lover* (1963), *Tea Party* (1965), *Landscape* (1968), *Night* (1969), *Silence* (1969), *Old Times* (1971), *Monologue* (1973) and *Betrayal* (1978) all deal with this subject to some extent.[1] In fact, it is difficult to find a drama by Pinter that does not take the concept into account at least in passing. Even Hirst and Spooner in *No Man's Land* (1975), for example, refer to their families (Spooner's malevolent mother, and his wife, who 'had everything. Eyes, a mouth, hair, teeth, buttocks, breasts.... And legs', and whom Hirst admits having seduced; Hirst's hazel-eyed wife).[2] Pinter's work in film provides a similar liturgy, witness *The Pumpkin Eater* (1964), *Accident* (1967), *The Go-Between* (1971), *Butley* (1973), *The Proust Screenplay* (1972) and *The French Lieutenant's Woman* (1981). However, it is not easy in examining all of these works to determine exactly either what Pinter's definition of family or his attitude toward the family might be, for each work displays unique elements, some of which, as might be expected in the dramatist's canon, produce contradictory statements.

This is true of *Family Voices*, one of Pinter's most recent plays, and one which may indicate that he is finally drawing some conclusions about the nature of 'family'. A radio play broadcast on B.B.C. Radio 3, 22 January 1981, *Family Voices* was subsequently staged in a 'platform performance' by the National Theatre in London on 13 February 1981, and then as one of a triptych under the common title *Other Places* (including *Victoria Station* and *A Kind of Alaska*) at the National Theatre in London on 14 October 1982. Along the lines of *Silence*, the play consists of a series of monologues spoken by three characters, two men and a woman. As in the earlier play, the three are separated, but in this case they are speaking about the present rather than the past, and while none hears the words of the others, the statements are directed to one another. The speakers are identified simply as Voice 1, Voice 2 and Voice 3. The only sound heard is their talk.

Voice 1 is a young man who seems to be reading aloud a letter that he has written to his mother. He describes the lodgings where he lives and the others who live there:

> ... my room is extremely pleasant. So is the bathroom. Extremely pleasant. I have some very pleasant baths indeed in the bathroom. So does everybody else in the house. They all lie quite naked in the bath and have very pleasant baths indeed.... the landlady ... is a Mrs. Withers, a person who turns out to be an utterly charming person....[3]

He concludes his letter affectionately, 'And so I shall end this letter to you, my dear mother, with my love.'[4]

The mother, Voice 2, also seems to be reading a letter aloud, one to her son asking why he never writes to her, inquiring about his life away from home, and informing him that his father has died. Interestingly, she seems to be writing at the same time as her son is, for she remarks that she does not have information that he has just mentioned in his letter:

> Darling. Where are you? The flowers are wonderful here. The blooms. You so loved them. Why do you never write? . . . Do you ever think of me? Your mother? Ever? At all? . . . Have you made friends with anyone?[5]

It is apparent that the two care for one another, and that they are trying to communicate; many of their comments are related, or at least parallel, yet there is never any connection. Occasionally, for instance, one says something that seems to be an answer to what the other has just said, but as the monologue continues it is clear that there has been no linkage, so the answer is not actually a response. It is, instead, merely that the two are talking about the same things. When the son observes, 'But I haven't forgotten that I have a mother and that you are my mother', for example, the second voices notes, 'Sometimes I wonder if you remember that you have a mother.'[6] This is not a reply, though, for the son goes on to describe having tea with Lady Withers and Jane, while the mother continues to wonder where her son has gone and why he never writes—even though ostensibly we are hearing him compose a letter to her all along. What develops is a picture of a parent and a child who care for one another and who think about one another, but who lead separate lives and never communicate their mutual thoughts and concerns, a fairly commonplace occurrence.

As noted above, the concept of family appears to some degree in almost everything that Pinter has written from *The Room* on, and throughout *Family Voices* phrases, lines, and passages echo from previous works to the extent that the play almost takes on the character of a self-parody. When Pinter has dealt with the idea of family before, his focus has been on one or the other of two sets of configurations, that of locus or that of relationship, though often the two are interconnected.

148

The locus set has to do with relationships between family members (family being defined either by blood or marital union) that are somehow tied to a particular location. For example, although *The Room* is not really about the concept of family and the legal relationship between Mr. and Mrs. Hudd serves merely as part of the setting and is not directly related to the play's meaning, still, Rose mothers her husband, Bert, in their room, and their relationship is clearly affected by her perception of the room as a sanctuary, a place where she and her younger husband will be safe and protected from outsiders.[7] Rose talks to her nonresponsive husband as though he were her young child:

ROSE. Here you are. This'll keep the cold out.

She places bacon and eggs on a plate, turns off the gas and takes the plate to the table.

It's very cold out, I can tell you. It's murder.

She returns to the stove and pours water from the kettle into the teapot, turns off the gas and brings the teapot to the table, pours salt and sauce on the plate and cuts two slices of bread. BERT *begins to eat.*

That's right. You eat that. You'll need it. You can feel it in here. Still, the room keeps warm. . . . Go on, Bert. Have a bit more bread. . . . I'll have some cocoa on when you come back.[8]

When Bert leaves the room, Rose makes sure that he is bundled up like a child going off to school:

ROSE. . . . Where's your jersey?

She brings the jersey from the bed.

Here you are. Take your coat off. Get into it.

She helps him into his jersey.

Right. Where's your muffler?

She brings a muffler from the bed.

Here you are. Wrap it round. That's it. Don't go too fast, Bert, will you? I'll have some cocoa on when you get back. You won't be long. Wait a minute. Where's your overcoat?[9]

In spite of the condescending tone and re-enforcing repetition used to reassure her husband, Rose's real concern is with their room, their sanctuary. Her husband's presence may be comforting, but her personal fear of whatever menace lies outside of their room is overriding, and it is this fear that is the focus of her attention, not the family itself. Rose constantly reminds both her husband and herself that 'The room keeps warm', and that 'you know where you are'[10] in such a place. In contrast, the outside world is dark, damp and cold. Only when Bert returns home, she insists, does he 'stand a chance'.[11]

Before Bert does return home, though, the doubly-dark blind, black man from the basement, Riley, intrudes upon Rose's sanctuary and proves her world vulnerable. Alluding to the family, Riley asks Rose to return home to her father.[12] As a result of her confrontation with this intruder, Rose goes blind. Bert returns home to the wife who took care of him, but whom he was unable to protect from the consequences of the outsider's intrusion.

Although in *The Birthday Party* Meg and Stanley are not related, she and her husband, Petey, treat their lodger as one of the family, at least in part because he has sought refuge in their boarding-house after having lost track of his father. Actually, Meg treats the middle-aged Stanley not just as one of the family, but as though he is a child. When he is late coming downstairs for breakfast, for example, Meg shouts up to him, 'Stan! . . . Stan! I'm coming up to fetch you if you don't come down! I'm coming up! I'm going to count three! One! Two! Three! I'm coming to get you!'[13] To get him out of bed she tickles him. Later, Meg arranges for Stanley's birthday party, where she gives him a toy drum, a child's toy. Meg's reaction after Goldberg and McCann have taken Stanley away to Monty, however, is subdued and self-centred: 'It was a lovely party. I haven't laughed so much for years. . . . I was the belle of the ball.'[14] The lodger was superficially made a member of the family merely because he was on the premises; when he goes only Petey seems to feel even the slightest bit of sadness. Ironically, some of the accusations levelled at Stanley by Goldberg have convinced critics to refer to Goldberg as a representative of the familial element in society—Stanley is derided for murdering his wife, for never having married, for deserting his pregnant fiancee, and for defiling his mother, among other things.[15]

In both *Night School* and *A Night Out* the protagonist is in a sense involved in a territorial battle with a relative.

In *Night School* when Walter returns home from prison he finds that his aunts have installed the school teacher Sally in his room and he has been relegated to a day-bed. His reaction is indignant:

> WALTER. A school teacher! In my room. . . . She's sleeping in my room!
> MILLY. What's the matter with the put-u-up? You can have the put-u-up in here.
> WALTER. The put-u-up? She's sleeping in my bed.
> ANNIE. She bought a lovely coverlet, she's put it on.
> WALTER. A coverlet? I could go out now, I could pick up a coverlet as good as hers. What are you talking coverlets for? . . . I can't believe it.[16]

Walter contends that he has a right to the room because it is his home, that he has lived in it for years, even having bought the bed that they are arguing about. Nevertheless, it is only after he has scared the girl away by threatening to expose her questionable background that he can regain his room. Family is less important to the aunts than is the rent money, and Walter never seems as upset about being displaced by his blood relations as he is with the physical loss of his place in the house. In this drama the definition of family includes no sense of responsibility, let alone belonging.

In *A Night Out* Albert's family situation is just the opposite of Walter's. Where Pinter explores the questions of a non-caring family with Walter, in the person of Albert he demonstrates what can happen when the family becomes too confining because it cannot let go of one of its members, when there is too much concern and affection. Albert tries to break his mother's apron-strings, in *A Night Out*, to escape from her house, but blood proves stronger than his sexual desires and he remains a member of a very non-extended family. In Act

One, when he breaks what appears to be a well-established pattern by announcing that he is going out for the evening to a party at a co-worker's, his mother shows her concern for his well-being, yet the questions that she asks reveal more than simply a mother's natural reaction to such news. 'You're not leading an unclean life, are you?' she wants to know, 'You're not messing about with girls, are you?'[17] When Albert returns from his misadventurous evening at the party and with the prostitute, his mother is waiting, and she consoles him:

> Do you know that time it is? . . . Where have you been? . . .
> Aren't I a good mother to you? Everything that I do is . . . is for
> your own good. You should know that. You're all I've got. . . .
> We'll have your holiday in a fortnight. . . . We can go away . . .
> together. . . . you're not a bad boy, Albert, I know you're
> not. . . . You're good, you're not bad, you're a good boy.[18]

In this play the lonely mother has smothered her 28-year-old son to the extent that he is forever bound to her. The drama's title re-enforces the metaphor of entrapment; Albert is stifled, constrained always to return home because of his mother's love.

Finally, *The Homecoming* serves as the culmination of the locus set, for Ruth's husband's family home functions both as a sanctuary and simultaneously a location where blood relatives constantly battle, where the place 'home' is ultimately defined by the relationships of those who live there rather than by kinship or the physical structure itself. Thus, Teddy is rejected and Ruth embraced because the concept of family likewise becomes defined by inter-relationships and not by blood or marriage. Home is where the family lives and the family group is established by individuals who fulfil each other's psychological needs.

There has been a definite evolution in Pinter's drama from *The Room* to *The Homecoming* in terms of the concept of 'home', as implied by the difference in the titles of the two plays. The word 'room' refers to a physical structure; the word 'homecoming' implies an emotional connotation. As I have said in *Butter's Going Up*, the movement reflected in the playwright's thinking is the difference between describing a symptom and discussing a disease. When, at the end of the play, Ruth says to the departing Teddy, 'Don't become a stranger',[19] she is stating the major theme of the drama. She does not dismiss Teddy as a person; rather, she rejects him as a member of a family that does not need her, and she needs to be needed. Therefore, while she opts to remain with her new family, as her Biblical forebear did in the Old Testament, because she fills a need and her needs are filled regardless of the lack of legal or blood connections, she and Teddy still can remain friends.

In plays in the relationship grouping, as in *The Homecoming*, it often seems as though the concept of family is almost coincidental. Frequently a family unit provides the characters and circumstances through which the playwright's themes can be developed and his subjects expressed naturally. At the same time, it is clear that the concept of family impinges on the themes, for the action grows out of the characters' familial relationships. In *A Slight Ache*, for instance, a husband is unable to satisfy his wife's needs, and, much as in *The Homecoming*, Flora rejects Edward and seeks out a substitute for him. The extent of Flora's desperation, like Lenny's in *The Homecoming*, is revealed by her reactions in the confrontation with the matchseller. He is described as being a mouldy, smelly, wet, muddy and sweating, 'great bollockfat of jelly',[20] yet she finds him sexually attractive and demands that he 'Speak to me of love.'[21] The play ends with Flora symbolically and literally exchanging her husband for the matchseller: '*She crosses to* EDWARD *with the tray of matches, and puts it in his hands. Then she and the* MATCHSELLER *start to go out as the curtain falls slowly.*'[22] As Pinter said in speaking of *The Homecoming*, 'If this had been a happy marriage it wouldn't have happened. . . . Certain facts like marriage and the family for this woman have clearly ceased to have any meaning.'[23] These words could be applied to Flora as easily as they were applied to Ruth.

How does Pinter define family, then, so that we know what it is that has ceased to have any meaning for these women? Well, in *The Caretaker* two brothers provide a partial answer. Their relationship is emphasized by the fact that they always refer to one another as 'brother', never by name, and Mick is his brother's keeper, even though Aston is the older of the two. When Davies intrudes and tries to come between them, the two men redefine their relationship. Mick's love and sense of responsibility coalesce with Aston's trust and appreciation for having been allowed to move toward self-sufficiency and self-confidence. This family unit survives intact and even is strengthened because the relationship has been reinterpreted in a way that recognizes potential disintegration, change and progress, and expels the disquieting agent. As Arnold P. Hinchliffe pointed out in his early study of Pinter, the final glance between the two brothers at the end of the play sums up what has happened, for it signifies that they have re-established the familial ties that bind them together, and also that they have united to reject the intruder.

The same kind of reaffirmation also takes place in *The Collection* and *The Lover*. In the first of these two dramas the family unit is disturbed because the husband, James, has begun to take his wife, Stella, for granted. The introduction of an outside force in the form of an alleged affair between Stella and Bill threatens the marriage in an even more dramatic way and forces James and Stella to re-establish their relationship with new bonds and with new understandings. With James's reassessment of the situation at play's end, Stella has clearly reversed the circumstances to the point that she emerges as the dominant partner, the one who will control the relationship from now on. James's hapless pleading and Stella's enigmatic response underscores their new positions:

JAMES. You didn't do anything, did you?

Pause.

He wasn't in your room. You just talked about it, in the lounge.

Pause.

That's the truth, isn't it?

Pause.

You just sat and talked about what you would do if you went to your room. That's what you did.

Pause.

Didn't you?

Pause.

That's the truth . . . isn't it?
>   STELLA *looks at him, neither confirming nor denying. Her face is friendly, sympathetic.*
>   *Fade flat to half light.*
>   *The four figures are still, in the half light.*
>   *Fade to blackout.*[24]

Whatever really happened is not significant. What is important is that the truth is that both James and Stella, in their own ways, are willing to fight to maintain their relationship.

In *The Lover* an imaginary lover leads another couple to reassess the basis on which their marital relationship exists, and to conclude that it is sound. This reaffirmation re-enforces their union because Richard no longer questions its fundamental appropriateness. Having found himself enmeshed in a game that was devised to strengthen the marriage but that has taken control of the couple's life, Richard informs his wife, Sarah, that the game must end: 'Perhaps you would give [Max, the imaginary lover, Richard's alter-ego] my compliments, by letter if you like, and ask him to cease his visits from (*He consults calendar.*)—the twelfth inst.'[25] The concept of family and marriage has been so important to this pair that they have been unable to reconcile their unrestrained, non-logical, passionate, sexual needs with their idealized definition of marriage (*vide* Richard's careful distinction between a wife, someone who is witty, respectable, dignified, admirable and full of sensibility, and whom he can love, and a mistress, someone who is 'handy between trains', who is 'a functionary who either pleases or displeases' by being able to 'express and engender lust with all lust's cunning'[26]). His attempt fails, though, and at the end of the play, while the marriage remains intact, it does so only because the couple is able to incorporate a new version of the game, symbolized by their costumes, into their lives.

>   SARAH. . . . Would you like me to change? Would you like me

to change my clothes? I'll change for you, darling. Shall I? Would you like that?

Silence. She is very close to him.

RICHARD. Yes.

Pause.

Change.

Pause.

Change.

Pause.

Change your clothes.

Pause.

You lovely whore.[27]

In *Tea Party*, however, Disson's jealousy centres on his bride and eventually leads to his nervous breakdown. He is suspicious of everyone; he cannot trust Diana, her brother, his sons, his parents, or his best man. The apparent betrayals here foreshadow those in the play *Betrayal*, written fifteen years later. In the later play every type of betrayal takes place: husband betrays wife, wife betrays husband, friend betrays friend, and business associate betrays business associate. Ironically, all of these betrayals are possible because of the interconnections that develop out of the context of Emma and Robert's marriage. Whereas the family has been a source of strength until now, in these plays it provides the cause for destruction, something implied but not realized heretofore.

Relationships between individuals, family members or otherwise, concerned Pinter up to this point. From here on his emphasis shifts. Relationships are still his subject, but they are examined through a gauze of time and memory—and the nature of reality, how relationships affect and are affected by time and memory, becomes the centre of his interest.

In *Landscape* a husband's infidelity drives his wife to retreat into a fantasy past from which he is unable to rescue her. In spite of Duff's alternate pleading and attempts to shock Beth, her psyche has been so damaged by his past action that he cannot move her from her idealized vision of her lover, but unlike the playacting engaged in in *The Lover*, Beth's vision is entirely imaginary. Her perfect marriage exists only in her mind.

Night features a married couple reminiscing about their first meeting, but their recollections do not mesh. This is somewhat like the differences in the descriptions of America given by Teddy and Ruth that serve to define the disparities in their needs in *The Homecoming*. The Man and the Woman both recall that they met at a party given by the Doughtys, but he remembers their first encounter as taking place on a bridge while she remembers it as having taken place by some railings in a field:

> MAN. I touched your breasts.
> WOMAN. Where?
> MAN. On the bridge, I felt your breasts.
> WOMAN. Really?
> MAN. Standing behind you.
> WOMAN. I wondered whether you would, whether you wanted to, whether you would.
> MAN. Yes.
>
>   .   .   .
>
> WOMAN. Another night perhaps. Another girl.
> MAN. You don't remember my fingers on your skin?
> WOMAN. Were they in your hands? My breasts? Fully in your hands?
> MAN. You don't remember my hands on your skin?
>
> *Pause.*
>
> WOMAN. Standing behind me?
> MAN. Yes.
> WOMAN. But my back was against the railings. I felt the railings . . . behind me. You were facing me. I was looking into your eyes. My coat was closed. It was cold.

MAN. I undid your coat.

WOMAN. It was very late. Chilly.

MAN. And then we left the bridge and we walked down the towpath and we came to a rubbish dump.

WOMAN. And you had me and you told me you had fallen in love with me, and you said you would take care of me always, and you told me my voice and my eyes, my thighs, my breasts, were incomparable, and that you would adore me always.

MAN. Yes I did.[28]

As in *The Collection*, the truth, the actual facts, of the original meeting are less important than the relationship established because of it, a relationship that led to a family and children and that has lasted.

Silence is the remembrance of how a marriage was prevented because of the nature of the individuals involved, individuals whose past relationships preclude the establishment of any new relationships. Rumsey, a man of 40, rejected Ellen, a woman in her twenties, because he felt that he was too old for her. Ellen in turn rejected Bates, a man in his thirties, because she could not marry Rumsey. Now the three remain isolated, alone in their rooms, remembering what they used to do together, imagining that they are still living those happier times. When their needs for a familial relationship were thwarted, the three characters became emotionally paralysed.

Pinter's best play, *Old Times*, recalls *The Caretaker* as an intruder attempts to come between a man and his wife, and Anna, like Davies before her, is expelled, the family remaining intact, albeit disturbed. *Old Times* illustrates the desperation of characters who attempt to restructure the past in order to provide themselves with a present in which they can establish a relationship that is vital to them. The husband and his wife's former room-mate discuss each other's marriages, infidelity, previous relationships, and promiscuity, all in order to devalue their opponent so that they can control Kate and either maintain or replace the other in a relationship with her. Anna's attempt to destroy the marriage fails, even though Deeley is not strong enough to repel her, because Kate wants the marriage to continue. During the last two or three minutes of the play no words are spoken, yet the emotional power generated by the characters' exposed needs is so great that the

158

audience is left overwhelmed. Deeley's sobbing reflects his sadness at having lost the sexual, passionate pleasures in life, his realization of his vulnerability, his recognition of Kate's power in contrast to his weakness, and his relief that he has been chosen to remain and that Kate has seen Anna 'dead' and, thus, the former room-mate can never threaten his marriage again.

Monologue is a short play in which a narrator remembers various relationships, including those in which he and his brother were involved. As with the characters in *Silence*, his experiences have left him isolated. The speaker's last words relate to a family that might have been. 'You could have had two black kids', the Man says, 'I'd have died for them. . . . I'd have been their uncle. . . . I am their uncle. . . . I'm your children's uncle. . . . I'll take them out, tell them jokes. . . . I love your children.'[29] And finally, in *Betrayal*, we look back through time to see how an adulterous affair evolved—and, as mentioned above, we see how everyone connected with a family is betrayed.

In this second set of plays the family is pivotal because it is the source of vulnerability. If the relationships survive whatever menaces them, they are revitalized and fortified. If the relationships cannot withstand the strain, not only does the family disintegrate but the individuals are cast into a no-man's-land of defeat, isolation and paralysis. When the family holds together, it is a source of strength; when it falls apart, individuals are left with nothing to support them. Kate remembers Anna dead, effectively excluding her from the family, and the voluble Anna for all intents and purposes is dead and never speaks again.

It is interesting, therefore, to note how *Family Voices* speaks out of the dramas that precede it, especially given the play's title. When the members of the family talk, they repeat sentiments from earlier plays. In this case location is unimportant, as suggested by the title, and the characters are concerned with their relationships with one another. In his first speech Voice 1 asks if his mother misses him, makes a joke, and describes those 'pleasant baths' taken by everyone in the house. The first two items are perfectly normal topics, but the depiction of the baths is reminiscent of Deeley's description

of Kate luxuriating in her bath in *Old Times* that is part of his
attempt to establish that his relationship with Kate is more
intimate and familial than Anna's. Voice 1 later exults that
he feels close to those who share a bathroom when he claims,
'I have found my home, my family. Little did I ever dream I
could know such happiness.'[30] Since this statement follows
his description of sharing tea with Lady Withers and Jane
and a recounting of his conversation with Riley, a fellow
lodger, while taking a bath, in which Riley explains how he
has turned away the inquiries of two women claiming to be
Voice 1's mother and sister by denying knowledge of him, it
can be assumed that the definition of family being dependent
upon blood relationship is supplanted here by a definition in
which emotional relationships are superior.

There are contradictory signals, however. First, Voice 1
claims that he is not lonely because, as in *Silence*, 'all that has
ever happened to me is with me, keeps me company; my
childhood, for example, through which you, my mother, and
he, my father, guided me.'[31] Then he talks of making new
friends, after which his mother, besides asking why he never
writes, wonders if he has made any nice friends, though like
Albert's mother in *A Night Out*, she is worried that he might
'get mixed up with the other sort', a good, motherly worry.[32]
Furthermore, in spite of Voice 1's admiration for those living
in the boarding-house, they seem a questionable lot. An old
man named Benjamin Withers, in spite of echoing Goldberg's
Polonius-like advice ('Keep your weight on all the left feet you
can lay your hands on. Keep dancing. . . . Mind how you go.
Look sharp. Get my drift? Don't let it get too mouldy.'[33]), is
summed up as someone 'to whom no one talks, to whom no
one refers, with evidently good reason'.[34] In *The Room* Riley
was the blind Negro who emerged from the basement calling
Rose Sal (Voice 1 is nicknamed Bobo by the other lodgers)[35]
and tells her that her father wants her to come home, then
switches to the first person, saying '*I* want you to come home'
(italics mine), a switch that Rose apparently does not notice,
implying that Riley might be her father. In *Family Voices* Riley
is the name of the bathroom conversationalist who sent the
two women packing (with a Davies-like 'Piss off out of it before
I call a copper'[36]) and who admires the bather's 'wellknit yet

slender frame' and admits that he fancies the younger man.[37] His descriptive phrases recall Flora's gushing over the match-seller in *A Slight Ache*. A self-avowed policeman who seldom leaves the house, he must be a 'secret policeman', Voice 1 concludes.[38] Mrs. Withers, who talks constantly about her experiences in the Women's Air Force during the Second World War, will not answer Voice 1's questions, but like Meg she entertains him and calls him her 'little pet'.[39] His comment on Jane, who wears black stockings and juggles buns with her toes, is that she 'continues to do a great deal of homework while not apparently attending any school'.[40] (There is also an echo of Spooner's remembrance of his mother's hot cross buns in *No Man's Land*.) Lady Withers wears a red dress (or maybe dark pink?), lives in an opulent apartment with 'sofas and curtains and veils and shrouds and rugs and soft material all over the walls, dark blue',[41] where she drinks rosé wine and plays the piano during the day. At night she receives guests who whisper on the stairs and in other rooms. Unlike T. S. Eliot's whisperers, who represent romantic love, these night whisperers are probably visiting a brothel. It is also important to realize that in the end, in the last words that he speaks, Voice 1 informs his mother that 'I am on my way back to you. I am about to make the journey back to you. What will you say to me?'[42]

Actually, it is easy to imagine what she will say. Throughout the play Voice 2 has repeated her questions—'Where are you? . . . Why do you never write? . . . Do you ever think of me?' She calls him 'Darling', reminds him that she is his mother, worries about his acquaintances, dreams of living 'happily ever after' with him and his young wife, remembers happy times together, recalls that she gave birth to him, curses him for abandoning her, assures him that she is waiting for him, reports his disappearance to the police, and wants to know if he thinks that 'the word love means anything'.[43] The some-times mutually exclusive statements are representative of the ambiguities in all of Pinter's work and, functioning as they do in the other plays, the contradictions are also a measure of how desperately Voice 2 needs to retain a familial relationship with her son and how destroyed she is without it. As if to emphasize this point, she also repeats a phrase that ties her reaction to the perceived loss of her son to the emotional sterility embraced by Hirst in *No Man's Land*: 'I sometimes think I have always been sitting like this, alone by an indifferent fire, curtains closed, night, winter.'[44] Moments later she is reminded of shampooing his hair and knowing simultaneously that he was 'entirely happy' in her arms while she was 'sitting by an indifferent fire, alone in winter, in eternal night without you'.[45] Past and present coexist and intrude upon one another, producing irony and a sense of prescience. All that is missing is Hirst's ice.

The third voice, which speaks only twice in the play, the first time after over 80% of the drama has transpired, is Voice 1's father. The intriguing thing about this, of course, is that it is on record that he is dead. He puts our minds at ease momentarily, saying that he is not dead, as his wife claimed three months ago, and Voice 2 did admit that she sometimes heard his cough and step upon the stair, though this could be dismissed as simply memories or imaginings kindled by the loss of a family member whose presence is missed, and how can a dead man talk anyway? But, then he admits,

> Well, that is not entirely true, not entirely the case. I'm lying. I'm leading you up the garden path, I'm playing about, I'm having my bit of fun, that's what. Because I am dead. As dead as a doornail. I'm writing to you from my grave. A quick word for old time's sake. Just to keep in touch. An old hullo out of the dark. A last kiss from Dad.[46]

Of course, although we only have his word for it, obviously Voice 3 would not lie to his son, although he just did, and a dead man would not lie, so he must actually be dead. This is reinforced by his statement that the only thing that he hears that breaks the absolute silence is the occasional barking of a dog—and this frightens him. Perhaps it is Cerberus?[47] So what is he doing writing letters if he is dead? His second speech, the final words spoken in the play, may hold the answer. His wife has reported that his deathbed reactions to his son were ambivalent—on one occasion she recounted that his last words were of tenderness[48]; elsewhere she describes his passing as in 'lamination and oath',[49] dying with a curse. He states that his son has prayed for his death 'from time immemorial', but he sends 'Lots of love', and encourages his son to 'keep up the good work', too.[50] The result of these contradictory statements is the lack of an unequivocal statement, something that has long been one of Pinter's trademarks, and it may be that he intends to connect ambivalence with the concept of family. The final words are 'I have so much to say to you. But I am quite dead. What I have to say to you will never be said.'[51] In 'The Love Song of J. Alfred Prufrock' Lazarus proclaims, 'I am Lazarus, come from the dead,/ Come back to tell you all, I shall tell you all.' But, Eliot's Lazarus, like the Biblical Lazarus, never says anything. Voice 3 holds out the promise of special knowledge, too, but he never reveals his secret.

One interpretation of *Family Voices* would be that the concept of family itself is dead. In a sense, though, this is probably moot. The play presents a series of disembodied voices who, because they are disembodied, cannot connect. The image that we are left with is one of separateness. Essentially, family has become a hollow concept. Everyone, even family members (whether related by blood, marriage, or emotional dependence), is isolated and lives speaking to others who cannot hear them, and hearing no one's voice but their own.

NOTES

1. In addition to the many play reviews of *The Lover* and *The Homecoming* (see my *Harold Pinter: An Annotated Bibliography* [Boston: G. K. Hall, 1978] for reference) and reviews of *Betrayal*, articles dealing with this aspect of Pinter's writing include: Thomas Adler, '*Night*: A Stroll Down Memory Lane' (*Modern Drama*, 17, 4 (December 1974), 461–65); John Arden, '*The Caretaker*' (*New Theatre Magazine*, 1, 4 [July 1960], 29–30); Steven M. L. Aronson, 'Pinter's "Family" and Blood Knowledge' (in *A Casebook on Harold Pinter's The Homecoming*, ed. John Lahr (New York: Grove, 1971), 67–86); Bernard F. Dùkore, 'A Woman's Place' (*Quarterly Journal of Speech*, 52, 3 (1967), 237–41, rpt. in Lahr's *A Casebook on Harold Pinter's The Homecoming*, 109–16); Gale, 'The Breakers of Illusion: George in Edward Albee's *Who's Afraid of Virginia Woolf?* and Richard in Harold Pinter's *The Lover*' (*Vision*, 1, 1 (Fall 1979), 70–7); Stuart Hall, 'Home Sweet Home', (*Encore*, 12 (July/August 1965), 30–4); Kelly Morris, 'The Homecoming' (*Tulane Drama Review*, 11, 2 (Winter 1966), 185–91); Hugh Nelson, '*The Homecoming*: Kith and Kin' (in *Modern*

British Dramatists: A Collection of Critical Essays, ed. John Russell Brown (Englewood Cliffs, N. J.: Prentice-Hall, 1968), 145–63); and R. F. Storch, 'Harold Pinter's Happy Families' (*Massachusetts Review*, 8 (August 1967), 703–12, rpt. in Arthur Ganz, *Pinter: A Collection of Critical Essays* (Englewood Cliffs, N. J.: Prentice-Hall, 1972), 136–46). Additional treatment of this subject may be found in Gale, *Butter's Going Up: A Critical Analysis of Harold Pinter's Work* (Durham N. C.: Duke University Press, 1977), Martin Esslin, *The Peopled Wound* (New York: Anchor, 1970), and Arnold P. Hinchliffe, *Harold Pinter* (New York: Twayne, 1967; rev. 1981).

2. Harold Pinter, *No Man's Land* in *Complete Works: Four* (New York: Grove, 1981), pp. 93, 127, 88.

3. *Family Voices*, in *Complete Works: Four*, pp. [281]–82.

4. Ibid., p. 183.

5. Ibid.

6. Ibid., p. 286.

7. See Gale, *Butter's Going Up*, for more extensive explications of *The Room* and the plays discussed below.

8. Pinter, *The Room*, in *Complete Works: One* (New York: Grove, 1976), pp. [101]–2.

9. Ibid., p. 110.

10. Ibid., pp. [101], 102.

11. Ibid., p. 105.

12. Ibid., pp. 124–25.

13. *The Birthday Party*, in Pinter, *Complete Works: One*, p. 23.

14. Ibid., p. 97.

15. Ibid., pp. 59–61.

16. *Night School*, in Pinter, *Complete Works: Two* (New York: Grove, 1977), pp. 204–5.

17. *A Night Out*, in *Complete Works: One*, p. 207.

18. Ibid., 244–47.

19. *The Homecoming* in Pinter, *Complete Works: Three* (New York: Grove, 1978), p. 96.

20. *A Slight Ache*, in *Complete Works: One*, p. 189.

21. Ibid., p. 192.

22. Ibid., p. 200.

23. Henry Hewes, 'Probing Pinter's Play', *Saturday Review*, 50 (8 April 1967), p. 58.

24. *The Collection*, in *Complete Works: Two*, p. 157.

25. *The Lover*, in *Complete Works: Two*, p. 190.

26. Ibid., pp. 167–69.

27. Ibid., p. 196.

28. *Monologue*, in *Complete Works: Four*, pp. 276–77.

29. *Night*, in *Complete Works: Three*, pp. 225–26.

30. *Family Voices*, p. 290.

31. Ibid., p. 282.

32. Ibid., p. 283.

33. Ibid., p. 291.

34. Ibid., p. 293.
35. Ibid., p. 295.
36. Ibid., p. 289.
37. Ibid., p. 292.
38. Ibid., p. 293.
39. Ibid., p. 285.
40. Ibid., p. 293.
41. Ibid., p. 286.
42. Ibid., p. 296.
43. Ibid.
44. Ibid., p. 289.
45. Ibid., p. 290.
46. Ibid., p. 294.
47. In the first American production, mounted by the American Repertory Theatre in March 1981 and directed by Michael Kustow, Voice 1 and Voice 2 were seated on chairs in separated areas of a darkened stage. The only light was a spotlight that was trained on whichever of the characters was speaking. The presence of Voice 3 was a *coup d' théâtre*, coming as a complete surprise. The actor was located in a third area of the stage, behind the first two and perhaps slightly elevated. When he spoke, a reddish spotlight was trained on his face from an oblique angle, focusing on the mouth and distorting the rest of his face. There was no doubt that the character was dead—though this was obviously a decision made by the stage director that did not have to be made by the director of the original radio version.
48. Ibid., p. 285.
49. Ibid., p. 287.
50. Ibid., p. 294.
51. Ibid., p. 296.

9

Alaskan Perspectives

by BERNARD F. DUKORE

Among the apparent atypicalities of *A Kind of Alaska* in the Pinter canon, as reviewers of the first production have been quick to observe, its programme note by the author, also a prefatory note to the play as published—*Other Places* (London: Methuen, 1982)—points to a literary source or inspiration: *Awakenings* by Oliver Sacks. Obviously, the chief—perhaps only—reason is to give credit where credit is due. Yet Pinter is so adept at concealing his tracks—unlike, say, Tennessee Williams, who in his later years spotlighted them—that one wonders whether he points in a certain direction partly in order to draw attention from another. I doubt that it takes much imagination to speculate whether Pinter, recently married at age 50, recalling the Pinter who had been newly married in his mid-twenties, used his own emotions as a creative springboard to draw the central figure of *A Kind of Alaska*, a middle-aged woman whose memory and part of her present is her younger self. From this supposition one may easily move to others. Consider Teddy's statement to his father, uncle, and brothers (*The Homecoming*): 'You wouldn't understand my works. You wouldn't have the faintest idea of what they were about.' Might this be an inversion of what adult Pinter heard from his boyhood friends when, after his success as a dramatist, he met them again? He certainly read such statements about his own 'works' from reviewers. For a writer as meticulous as Pinter, it can hardly be accidental that the people to whom Teddy speaks 'wouldn't appreciate the

166

points of reference'. Perhaps like critics of Pinter's early plays (and—why not?—later as well) those whom Teddy addresses are 'way behind'. One may also wonder the extent to which Stanley's account of responses to his piano recital (*The Birthday Party*) draws upon experiences of Pinter when he was a young actor.

The foregoing is certainly not to say that these characters are simply autobiographical. To cite one difference per play, unlike the character in the first Pinter is a man; unlike the figure in the second he has no brothers; unlike that in the third he is not a pianist. These personages are fictitious. Yet (axiomatically) the characters, situations and emotions a writer creates derive from his own experiences, emotions, observations and readings (which may be no less important to him than other, supposedly more personal experiences). One's interest in an artistic product leads to interest in its producer. Speculations or inferences like those in the previous paragraph are therefore inevitable. Although Pinter is entitled to his privacy, which will not be invaded by the like of me (apart from not having met him, I am temperamentally incapable of filling the rôle of gossip columnist), understanding of an artist's life sometimes leads to a clearer understanding of his art.

There is a point to these conjectures or ruminations—pronounced roominations, thus coincidentally linking Pinter's recent play, *A Kind of Alaska*, with his first, *The Room*, a play whose nonliterary genesis he also noted (two men he observed, one silent while the other chattered on). An apparently atypical work can suggest perspectives with which to regard other, more obviously typical works.

As quick as reviewers have been to recognize that it is unusual for Pinter to reveal a play's source, they have been equally quick to notice an uncharacteristic feature of the play itself, a psychological study of a woman in her mid-forties, Deborah, who through injection of the recently discovered drug L-DOPA awakens from sleeping sickness, which she contracted when a teenager. For Pinter, the situation is surprisingly clearcut and the ambiguities of a teenage consciousness in a mature woman's body receive an unambiguous explanation. We watch the tensions between two-people-in-one, a girl's response to her woman's body and to a fresh

167

world, her unpractised efforts to conceal and to cope. After the play opened in London at the Cottesloe Theatre, the smallest of the National Theatre's three houses, on 14 October 1982, standard reactions included: 'the reality of the situation' marks 'a departure for Mr. Pinter' (Robert Cushman, *Observer*); 'He was never less obscure than here' (John Barber, *Daily Telegraph*); 'a new surge of realism', the play is 'more nakedly dramatic and certainly more accessible than anything he has written before' (Jack Tinker, *Daily Mail*); and 'Pinter, uncharacteristically, has chosen to write what is almost a documentary study of a patient recovering from sleeping sickness' (John Elsom, *Sunday Mail*).

Does *A Kind of Alaska* really represent a radical departure for Pinter? Despite the play's semblance of atypicality, its vista is that Pinterland to which a quarter of a century has accustomed us. The newly awakened girl-woman's complaint, on the second page of the printed text, 'No one is listening to me', echoes those works of Pinter in which characters, not listening to each other, talk at cross-purposes. The doctor's question that prompts her complaint, 'Who am I?', reiterated immediately after Deborah's lament by the more precise query, 'Do you know who I am?', repeats similar questions asked by other characters in Pinter's plays, for example: 'Tell me, Mrs. Boles, when you address yourself to me, do you ever ask yourself who exactly you are talking to?' (*The Birthday Party*); 'Do you know me?' (*The Collection*); 'I know him.' 'Do you really?' (*No Man's Land*).

In *A Kind of Alaska*, metaphysical resonances on the subject of identity seem to diminish. Does not the programme and prefatory note explain the situation, thereby accounting for the dialogue and permitting one to accept such questions at their face value? Take what would otherwise be Pinter's almost trademarked ambiguities, wherein a flat statement calls into question equally unambiguous assertions. Says Deborah:

I am twelve. No. I am sixteen. I am seven.

Pause.

I don't know. Yes. I know. I am fourteen. I am fifteen. I'm lovely fifteen.

Our knowledge of what her situation is makes the statements of the awakened Deborah comprehensible. As the unfortunate girl-woman says, she does not know—though she immediately contradicts herself on this point. Despite her assertiveness, she guesses. We can see for ourselves that the 16-, 7-, 14-, or as she reiteratively concludes 15-year-old girl—who her sister later says was 16 when sleeping sickness struck—is in her mid-forties. The accuracy of her guesses does not matter. What matters is what happens; she herself in the present tries to ascertain the truth. This is part of the action of *A Kind of Alaska*, as it is of other plays by Pinter, in which what happens is dramatically more important than what happened. By placing his customary techniques and themes in what for him is a generally different context, the known or understandable, one might infer that one should observe earlier plays with them in ways similar to one's observation of *A Kind of Alaska*. I say 'generally different' because he uses a related stratagem in another play, the relatively recent *Betrayal*, wherein the backward moving dramatic action gives us, though not the characters, a known or understandable context.

A Kind of Alaska provides the imprecise, unexplainable, unknown, or unremembered in a context that does not prompt spectators or readers to ask what really happened but rather to understand that certain matters are imprecise, inexplicable, unknown, or unremembered. See, for instance, this partly comic dialogue between doctor and patient:

> HORNBY. You fell asleep and no one could wake you. But although I use the word sleep, it was not strictly sleep.
> DEBORAH. Oh, make up your mind.
>
> *Pause.*
>
> You mean you thought I was asleep but I was actually awake?
> HORNBY. Neither asleep nor awake.
> DEBORAH. Was I dreaming?
> HORNBY. Were you?
> DEBORAH. Well was I? I don't know.

Deborah's last two speeches unquestionably demonstrate the unreliability of memory—a familiar Pinter theme. Note, however, the difference between our response to them and our responses to such passages as Stanley's recollection of his concert (*The Birthday Party*), Aston's account of his medical experience (*The Caretaker*), and both versions of seeing *Odd Man Out* (*Old Times*). While one might wonder the extent to which the victim of sleeping sickness was aware of what occurred about her while she slept or seemingly slept and while one might wonder about her dreams, which she claims not to remember, one does not question the accuracy of her claim—partly because of context, partly because few of us without sleeping sickness remember our dreams, and partly because those of us who remember them do not always do so.

In short, the unfamiliar yet familiar qualities of *A Kind of Alaska* suggest perspectives with which to regard Pinter's earlier plays. Just as we accept the doctor's inability to pinpoint the states of sleep, awake, and 'not strictly sleep', and just as the awakened Deborah does not know whether she dreamt, we may assume that the past is as imprecise and as unremembered for people who have not had sleeping sickness.

After all, as a voice-over says at the start of Pinter's movie adaptation of *The Go-Between*, a line that also begins L. P. Hartley's original novel, 'The past is a foreign country. They do things differently there.' Deborah's past is a foreign country which she no longer inhabits. In Dr. Hornby's words, her mind 'took up a temporary habitation . . . in a kind of Alaska'. She dwelt in frozen isolation in what Pinter calls in another play, whose title is the first phrase, 'no man's land. Which never moves, which never changes, which never grows older, but which remains forever, icy and silent.' *It* may never change, but its sojourner, however long he or she may remain there, changes. If nothing else, the resident ages. While the change is gradual, short periods of time lengthen: moment by moment, day by day, year by year, decade by decade. The Alaska-like deep freeze, a no-man's-land, is therefore both unchanging and temporary. One's view of it now differs from one's earlier view. Even Deborah's does, for she is no longer there and she has a different body. Now, that icy, silent past or Alaska or no-man's-land is a foreign country. What does one remember of it? Has one's memory altered the actuality? Notice how a statement by the woman in *Silence* partly resembles Deborah's position: 'I'm never sure that what I remember is of to-day or of yesterday or of a long time ago.' What we accept at face value in *A Kind of Alaska* suggests that we might similarly accept statements in other plays by Pinter.

A Kind of Alaska is not a touchstone that enables us to regard Pinter's earlier plays in a simplistic way, as this proposal might appear. The new play's complexities raise questions about it and prompt further questions about Pinter's other plays. For example, more than halfway through the action Deborah becomes aware of a third person in the room, Pauline, who introduces herself as Deborah's sister. Only at this time does Pinter alert the reader to her presence. Does the spectator first see her then or is she visible from the start? Pinter does not say. Nor do reviews of the first production. Directors of future productions must decide. They should also decide whether lights unobtrusively intensify on her when Deborah becomes aware of her or whether she steps into a lighted area to make Deborah aware of her. All that Pinter's printed text reveals is that Hornby is not cognizant of Pauline's presence until Deborah is. 'I didn't call you', he tells Pauline; but he permits her to speak to Deborah. Soon comes this crucial exchange:

> PAULINE. Shall I tell her lies or the truth?
> HORNBY. Both.

The sympathy with which one views the situation or the empathy one has with Deborah should not obscure the fact that what Pauline tells her, and implicitly what Hornby has told and will tell her, may be untrue.

Again we are on familiar Pinter terrain, the *terra incognita* that custom has made *terra cognita*—but with a difference that also exists, too often overlooked, in Pinter's other drama, as it does in the world his drama reflects. While people unconsciously distort the truth, for as much Pinter criticism reminds us their views are limited and their memories fallible, they also consciously lie. The performance implications of these factors are vital. Since a great deal has been written on ambiguities, unconscious distortions, and the like, I wish to focus on the issue of conscious lies. 'I am a widow', Pauline tells Deborah, a seemingly clearcut statement of fact. But is it? For us, there may be as much ambiguity in that statement as there is between sleep and wakefulness; but Pauline herself knows the truth. Two pages later, Hornby tells Deborah, referring to Pauline, 'When she was twenty I married her. She is a widow. I have lived with you.' Is she a widow because her husband has spent so much time away from her, caring for Deborah, that he has made her a *de facto* widow? Or was she a widow when they married? If so, her first husband would have died when she was extremely young and both her and Hornby's use of the present tense would, to say the least, be odd, considering that their marriage would have lasted some twenty years (Pauline is four years younger than Deborah). If the former is the case, Pauline's statement about her widowhood, literally untrue, may be intended more for Hornby than for Deborah and Hornby's support of that statement may be an attempt to clarify their relationship for Deborah's benefit and perhaps also to confess to his wife his understanding of what he has done to her. But might Hornby lie about the marriage? If Pauline is a widow in the conventional sense of the term, the lie and the statement 'I have lived with you' could be efforts to reassure Deborah by conveying a sense of familial stability. Although the actors would be clear in their own minds as to which assertions are true, which lies, and what meanings the true statements have, they might opt for a result of ambiguity or they might choose to let us know clearly the difference between the characters' truths and lies. Different interpretations result in different line readings, and at least in this section of the play the characters' relationships and motivations have widely diverse possibilities.

We have become so accustomed to ambiguities in both performance and criticism of Pinter's plays that now might be an appropriate time to consider production possibilities of the clearcut. From Pinter's very recent play, let us turn to his first. In *The Room*, Kidd mentions his sister. After he leaves, Rose's first words are, 'I don't believe he had a sister, ever.' Is she lying in order to create conversation with Bert? Should the actress make us aware that she lies? If Rose tells the truth, is she correct? Did she hold this belief before Kidd entered or did she acquire it during the scene in which he comments on his sister? Does Kidd consciously lie? If he does, does the actor who plays the rôle make us aware he is doing so? Whether or not he lies, does Rose make us aware of her disbelief? Does Kidd become aware of it? His first reference to his sister is in a context of his younger days, when he was more fit than he is now:

> That was when my sister was alive. But I lost track a bit, after she died. She's been dead some time now, my sister. It was a good house then. She was a capable woman. Yes. Fine size of a woman too. I think she took after my mum. Yes, I think she took after my old mum, from what I can recollect. I think my mum was a Jewess. Yes, I wouldn't be surprised to learn that she was a Jewess. She didn't have many babies.

If Rose expresses disbelief and makes Kidd aware of it, and if such expression and awareness occur after, let us suppose, the first and then second sentences, these affect the interpretation of the third sentence, which could be an effort to persuade Rose that the sister is dead. Or it could mean that while he really had a sister he cannot prove it to Rose because she is dead. Or he could invent lie upon lie to make Rose believe he had a sister. There are other possibilities: he could be oblivious to Rose's disbelief and either ramblingly reminisce about his real sister or continue to invent lies without being aware that Rose does not believe him; or Rose might not express her disbelief but instead egg him on. Is his mother's possible Judaism a lie, an inference, a reference to his sister's religion, or a shift of subject with no relationship to his sister? Did his sister have many or any children? In fact, does he in this instance refer to her or to his mother? One could continue at greater length, of course, but the point is that the reading of these passages and the reaction to them derive from answers to Pauline's question, 'Shall I tell her lies or the truth?'—an implication that the speaker can differentiate between them— and from the other characters' belief or disbelief—which may have a similar implication (it does for Rose, does not for Deborah). In *The Room*, Rose's four speeches that follow the quotation about Kidd's sister are all questions and all refer to her: 'What about your sister, Mr. Kidd?' 'Did she have any babies?' 'When did she die then, your sister?' 'What did she die of?' Kidd answers none of them. During the interplay between him and Rose, the issues of whether he lies about having had a sister, whether Rose does not believe him at that time, and whether she expresses her disbelief then are not merely academic. They affect the performance and through it our perception of the play. To tell the truth, I cannot definitively answer my own questions. Yet different answers will result in different performances, thus different interpretations of the play.

In *The Caretaker*, Mick at one point tells Davies 'Most of what you say is lies.' 'Most', not 'All'. Perhaps following Hornby's advice to Pauline, Davies sometimes tells the truth, sometimes (or most of the time) lies. While his appearance makes it difficult to credit his assertion, 'I'm clean. I keep myself up', his story of the monk who told him (in his paraphrase) 'If you don't piss off [. . .] I'll kick you all the way to the gate' might conceivably be true. So might his tale of having refused to remove a bucket of rubbish on the basis that such work was not part of his job. Davies' alternation of truth and lies, each related in a different manner, would add variety, perhaps enrichment, to the performance of this character.

Take a scene in which no one refers to or accuses a man of lying. In *The Homecoming*, Ruth demands a flat that has a bedroom, a dressing-room, and a room to rest. After a pause:

> LENNY. All right, we'll get you a flat with three rooms and a bathroom.
> RUTH. With what kind of conveniences?
> LENNY. All conveniences.
> RUTH. A personal maid?
> LENNY. Of course.
>
> *Pause.*
>
> We'd finance you, to begin with, and then, when you were established, you could pay us back, in instalments.
> RUTH. Oh, no, I wouldn't agree to that.
> LENNY. Oh, why not?
> RUTH. You would have to regard your original outlay simply as a capital investment.
>
> *Pause.*
>
> LENNY. I see. All right.
> RUTH. You'd supply my wardrobe, of course?

LENNY. We'd supply everything. Everything you need.
RUTH. I'd need an awful lot. Otherwise I wouldn't be content.
LENNY. You'd have everything.
RUTH. I would naturally want to draw up an inventory of everything I would need, which would require your signatures in the presence of witnesses.
LENNY. Naturally.
RUTH. All aspects of the agreement and conditions of employment would have to be clarified to our mutual satisfaction before we finalized the contract.
LENNY. Of course.

Pause.

RUTH. Well, it might prove a workable arrangement.
LENNY. I think so.

By now, we as audiences and readers are familiar with the virtues of ambiguity in this scene, of the open question as to who dominates or would dominate whom, of the possibility that Ruth raises the ante to see how far she can go, of the interpretation that Ruth is queen bee in this previously all male household, and so forth. But suppose that through intonation and interplay Lenny shows us that he lies, that he has no intention of submitting to her demands, and that he is confident that with Teddy gone he can make Ruth, now older than when she 'was a model for the body. A photographic model for the body' (and her clarification may be true, may be a lie to disguise her participation in a far older profession, of which 'model for the body' may be a euphemism), conform to his demands. Apart from the results in the actor who reads Lenny's speeches, this interpretation would have results in the actress who reads Ruth's. As a consequence, the implications of Lenny's silence when Max expresses alarm that Ruth will 'do the dirty on us, you want to bet? She'll use us, she'll make use of us, I can tell you! I can smell it!' would be affected, as would the final tableau.
Tea Party has a simpler situation. After Disson and Diana marry, the scene shifts from the wedding reception to a hotel room where the newlyweds are in bed together. The scene is brief:

175

DISSON. Are you happy?
DIANA. Yes.
DISSON. Very happy?
DIANA. Yes.
DISSON. Have you ever been happier? With any other man?
DIANA. Never.

Pause.

DISSON. I make you happy, don't I? Happier than you've ever been . . . with any other man.
DIANA. Yes. You do.

Pause.

Yes.

Silence.

Does Diana lie? If so, does she lie to one or both sets of questions (being happy and having been happier with another man)? In either case, might she make us aware that she lies? Pinter does not say. The printed text is the script for television, where *Tea Party* was first performed. The author specifies: *'The light is on. The camera rests at the foot of the bed. The characters are not seen. Their voices heard only.'* One may infer that Pinter intends ambiguous answers to my questions. When *Tea Party* was produced on stage—first in New York, then in London—ambiguity was achieved. One could take Diana's responses either way, for the actress's speech was neutral. The focus became Disson's insecurities that lead to his deterioration. One did not clearly know the extent to which his imaginings were justified. Both stage productions were extremely effective (I did not see the televised version). But suppose one ignores what is merely inferred authorial intention and imagines that Diana lies to one or both sets of questions and lets us know she lies. The play may become richer if one perceives at least some justification for Disson's fears. Richer or not, the production would differ from both that I saw, and I am curious as to how this factor would affect other key scenes and our general perception of the play's dramatic action and conclusion.

I do not argue for simplistic interpretation. Rather, I propose that Pauline's question be asked of all Pinter's characters, together with the questions of whether the characters reveal deceit to the audience and whether other characters recognize they hear lies. To tell the truth once more, I do not know what the results would be. However, I can guess that they would differ from what one may call traditionalist ambiguity in productions of Pinter's plays. They might provide additional insights to his work, from *The Room* to *A Kind of Alaska*.

Notes on Contributors

ALAN BOLD was born in 1943 in Edinburgh where he attended university and trained as a journalist. Since 1966 he has been a full-time writer and visual artist and since 1975 has lived in rural Fife writing books and contributing features regularly to the *Scotsman* and occasionally to the *New Statesman, T.L.S., Glasgow Herald* and *Tribune.* He has published many books of poetry including *To Find the New, The State of the Nation* and a selection in *Penguin Modern Poets 15.* His *In This Corner: Selected Poems 1963–83* represents his best work over the past two decades; with the artist John Bellany he has collaborated on *A Celtic Quintet* and *Haven.* He has edited many anthologies including *The Penguin Book of Socialist Verse, The Martial Muse,* the *Cambridge Book of English Verse 1939–75, Making Love, The Bawdy Beautiful, Mounts of Venus, Drink To Me Only, The Poetry of Motion.* He has also written critical books on *Thom Gunn and Ted Hughes, George Mackay Brown, The Ballad, Modern Scottish Literature* and *MacDiarmid: The Terrible Crystal.* He has edited *The Thistle Rises: A MacDiarmid Miscellany* and *The Letters of Hugh MacDiarmid.* He has exhibited his Illuminated Poems (pictures combining an original poetic manuscript with an illustrative composition) in venues as varied as Boston University and the National Library of Scotland.

KATHERINE H. BURKMAN, an Associate Professor of English at the Ohio State University, was born in Chicago in 1934. Her B.A. is from Radcliffe College, her M.A. in English from the University of Chicago, and her Ph.D. in Theatre from the Ohio State University. She has published several articles on Modern Drama and has written *The Dramatic World of Harold Pinter: Its Basis in Ritual* (1971), and *Literature as Performance: Shakespeare's Mirror and a Canterbury Caper* (1978). She is presently working on a book on modern drama, *The Arrival of Godot.*

CHARLES A. CARPENTER, Professor of English at the State University of New York at Binghamton, was born in 1929 and completed his Ph.D. in English at Cornell University in 1963. He has published a study of Shaw's early plays, *Bernard Shaw and the Art of Destroying Ideals* (1969), a Goldentree bibliography of modern British drama (1979), and many articles, including four on Pinter's plays. He has contributed annual bibliographies of modern drama studies to the journal *Modern Drama* since 1974 and recently completed his *International Bibliography of Modern Drama Scholarship and Criticism, 1966–1980.*

BERNARD F. DUKORE is Professor of Drama and Theatre at the University of Hawaii. His books include *American Dramatists 1918–1945* (1984), *Harold Pinter* (1982), *The Theatre of Peter Barnes* (1981), and *The Collected Screenplays of Bernard Shaw* (1980).

STANLEY EVELING was born in Newcastle-upon-Tyne in 1925 and came to Scotland, in 1960, to teach philosophy at Edinburgh University. He is the author of several plays, including *Come and Be Killed* (1967), and contributes a weekly television column to the *Scotsman*.

STEVEN H. GALE was born in San Diego, California in 1940. He received his B.A. degree in English from Duke University (1963), his M.A. from the University of California at Los Angeles (1965), and his Ph.D. from the University of Southern California (1970). In 1980 he moved to Missouri Southern State College to become Professor and Head of the Department of English there. Currently he is directing the college's campus-wide Honors Program/Interdisciplinary Studies Program, which he developed in 1984. Among his publications are *Butter's Going Up: A Critical Analysis of Harold Pinter's Work* (1977), which was nominated for the *Explicator*, American Theatre Association, and California Literature Medal literary awards, and the standard Pinter bibliography, *Harold Pinter: An Annotated Bibliography* (1978). He is also the editor of *Harold Pinter: Critical Approaches* (1985). In addition, among his forty-five published articles are eleven essays on Pinter.

SIR PETER HALL, born in Suffolk in 1930, succeeded Lord Olivier as Director of the National Theatre of Great Britain in March 1973 and was appointed Artistic Director of Glyndebourne in January 1984. He has been Director, Oxford Playhouse (1954–55), Director, Arts Theatre, London (1955–57) and Managing Director, Royal Shakespeare Company (1960–68). He has directed over sixty major theatre productions in London, Stratford-upon-Avon and New York, including nineteen Shakespeare plays and the premieres of plays by

Pinter, Beckett, Tennessee Williams, Albee, Anouilh, Peter Shaffer, John Mortimer, John Whiting and Alan Ayckbourn. He has also directed opera at Covent Garden, Sadler's Wells and Glyndebourne and eight films including Pinter's *The Homecoming* (1973). He is Associate Professor of Drama at Warwick University and has honorary doctorates from York, Reading, Liverpool, Leicester, Cornell U.S.A.

RONALD KNOWLES was born in 1940 and raised in London. He attended University College, Swansea, the Warburg Institute, and Birkbeck College, University of London. Since 1971 he has been a lecturer in English at the University of Reading. He has published several studies of Pinter's work.

RANDALL STEVENSON was born in 1953 in the north of Scotland, and grew up in Glasgow. He attended Edinburgh University, where he won the James Elliot Prize. After a year teaching English in a training college in North-West State, Nigeria, he returned to post-graduate study at the University of Oxford. He is now a lecturer in English literature, with particular responsibility for drama, at the University of Edinburgh. He has published work on William Faulkner, Charles Dickens, Thomas Pynchon, and Giles Gordon, and reviews theatre occasionally for B.B.C. Radio, the *Times Literary Supplement*, and *Cencrastus*.

Index

Index